Wines of the Midwest

Books by Ruth Ellen Church

The American Guide to Wines
Entertaining with Wine
Favorite American Wines and How to Enjoy Them
Wines of the Midwest

Wines
of the
Midwest

Ruth Ellen Church

Swallow Press/Ohio University Press
Chicago Athens, Ohio London

Library of Congress Catalog Card Number: 77-83753
ISBN 0-8040-0779-9 clothbound
ISBN 0-8040-0426-9 paperbound

Swallow Press Books
are published by
Ohio University Press
Athens, Ohio 45701

Table of Contents

The New Grapes of the Midwest and Their Growers

Climate is the determinant of all grape growing—more important than the choice of grape varieties because it has the last word on what varieties can, and cannot be grown.

—Philip Wagner

In a nutshell, that's the big problem with wine-growing in the East and Midwest. The classical wine grapes which thrive in California—white riesling, chardonnay, pinot noir, cabernet sauvignon, and others—are very difficult to grow where winters are long and cold. A few of the hardier native grapes, notably the delaware and catawba, do make acceptable wine, but most make wine that is not enjoyed by anyone who is accustomed to the subtler flavors and aromas of wines from California and Europe.

The concord grape, a native variety of the **labrusca** family, thrives in the Midwest. It makes marvelous pie, grape juice, and jam, but is a grape so high in acid that it must be diluted generously with water and loaded with sugar to make a drinkable wine. Even then, given today's sophisticated palate, such wine is rarely acceptable.

To improve wines from native grapes in the Midwest and East, the big wineries have learned to blend their wines with some of California's excess production. Konstantin Frank, who grows white (Johannisberg) riesling and other classic grapes on the shores of Keuka Lake in New York's Finger Lakes district, has proven that they'll grow in protected areas (a big body of water is excellent protection) where the thermometer seldom hits zero, and the winds of winter are not too fierce. Frank has an enthusiastic following.

However, most authorities doubt that growing classic vinifera grape varieties will prove to be economically sound where the growing season is short and the endemic vine diseases are rampant. Few of the new winegrowers east of the Mississippi can resist giving it a try. To their later chagrin, two- or three-year-old vines, which they've nurtured tenderly, are sometimes lost in a sudden freeze. Ultimately, the question will be settled by experience.

If native grapes make coarse wine, and classic grapes are not sufficiently rugged and disease resistant to survive Midwestern winters and summers, what is the answer? The answer is fascinating, because it is bringing to American wine glasses a whole new range of wines without the unpleasant characteristics evident in wine from native grapes. They are wines from grapes well adapted to rigorous climates, their vines resistant to disease. The grapes are known as French hybrids in the United States and Canada, and as American hybrids in France, where most of them were developed.

Most of them are not new, but only in the last decade have they become a powerful impetus to winegrowing. They fit the back-to-nature movement and trend of the times, which is toward serving wine instead of stronger drink at parties, and accompanying meals with wine.

Most of the hybrids now being planted widely in the Midwest were developed by French growers following the terrible phylloxera scourge of the last century, which laid waste Europe's vineyards. They discovered that it was possible to re-establish vineyards by grafting the delicate classic vines onto sturdy, disease-resistant American rootstocks. The grapes kept their own natural characteristics; they did not take on any of the rougher qualities of grapes which might have been expected to come from the grafted roots.

Then, these French investigators experimented with true crosses between grape species in order to find vines adapted to many different growing conditions, the fruits of which would make good wine.

Some made thousands of experiments, of which only a few were successful. "Poor Maurice Baco!" I heard a Midwestern grower say. "He made ten thousand crosses and his very first one was the best!" That was Baco No. 1, now called **baco noir**. It makes an excellent red wine in the Midwest.

Most hybrid vines still are known by their numbers, but many have been given names. Sometimes the developer's name is lost in the process. For example, Seibel 10878 is now called **chelois**, and Joannes-Seyve 26205* is **chambourcin**. These grapes were named in France. But some names were bestowed in 1970 by the Finger Lakes Wine Growers Association. **Cascade**, for example, which has an American ring, was formerly known as Seibel 13053.

In the development and use of French-American hybrid vines in the United States there is a key figure, Philip Wagner, whose words open this chapter. A former editor of the *Baltimore Sun*, Wagner was instrumental in bringing hybrid vines to the United States soon after the end of Prohibition. In partnership with his wife Jocelyn, Wagner established a nursery for hybrid stock and a small winery in Riderwood, Maryland, which they thought of as essentially a demonstration project, to show that good wines could be produced from such grapes in areas where wine had not previously been produced. In addition to providing the raw materials for establishing scores of new vineyards, the Wagners developed their own Boordy wines, which were produced on their Maryland estate. In 1980 the Wagners sold their wine business to associates, but retained the nursery.

Philip Wagner's book *A Wine Grower's Guide* has helped, in its several editions, to establish many of the Midwest's vineyards and wineries. Bernard Rink, who opened his Boskydel Vineyard in northern Michigan in 1976, took his inspiration from the Wagner book as much as twelve years earlier, when he planted twenty acres experimentally, five to ten vines each of thirty hybrid varieties, from which he was able to select the six hybrids best adapted to the microclimate of his water-blessed location.

Growers and winemakers help each other, and there is much help available from state experiment stations such as the New York Agricultural Experiment Station at Geneva, the Western Ohio Experiment

---

* The numbers do not necessarily indicate the number of seedlings. This set of numbers indicates seedling number 205 in row 26.

Station at Wooster, the work being done at State College, Pennsylvania, and at the University of California at Davis.

The American Wine Society brings grape farmers and winemakers together to discuss their many problems at annual seminars, and *Eastern Grape Grower and Winery News Magazine* sponsored its first "Wineries Unlimited" technical seminar in 1976, which led to the organization of the Association of American Vintners in 1978, with some 170 members in twenty-eight states. There is an eastern section of the American Society of Enologists who deal with the special problems of winemaking east of the Rocky Mountains.

Plenty of advice and assistance is available, but in the long run, each vineyard is a law unto itself. The vines that thrive in one particular vineyard may not do well in another only a few miles away.

Establishing a winery is not easy. The William Welsch family of Fenn Valley Vineyards looked for three years in six states before settling upon their location near Lake Michigan's eastern shore. Once found, the land must be cleared and planted experimentally to see which vines grow best. These vines must be staked, wired, pruned at the right time, sprayed against insect pests, and protected from animal pests. Along the way, some of man's best friends may become enemies—birds, bees, bunnies, and deer among them. Birds may devour a first crop before it can be harvested.

It is all hard work and far from immediately rewarding, as grape vines do not produce crops until the third or fourth year. It is a commonly held concept that one should not plant grapes with a view to establishing a winery without financial resources to cover ten years. While waiting for vines to produce, it is usual for growers to buy grapes from others to make their early wines.

Wine people, as a group, seem to be the happiest people in the world. Some are young, enthusiastic, well-educated couples who find joy in working with nature. Others are successful businessmen who have made their mark and now want to put their money into an enterprise that will give them personal satisfaction for the rest of their lives.

Some of the grapes they are finding most successful for Midwestern vineyards are described in the following list. The names are daily becoming more familiar on wine labels. Also included are two shorter lists of native and classic varieties grown in the Midwest.

Hybrid Wine Grapes
of the Midwest

For White Wines

Aurora: Hardy, productive, early ripening. An excellent all-around grape for clean, fresh, rather neutral white wine made with or without residual sweetness. Aging in oak brings out flavor.

Cayuga: A grape developed at the New York Agricultural Station, Geneva, by crossing the seyval blanc with an earlier grape developed at Geneva, the Schuyler. It makes excellent wine in New York and is now being planted experimentally in the Midwest.

Ravat 51 or Vignoles: Having a chardonnay parent, this grape could make a more authentic "chablis" than is generally made in the United States (France's chablis is made of chardonnay). The wine is clean and crisp.

Rayon d'Or: Formerly known as Seibel 4986, the vine is hardy and productive. The wine is of dependably high quality, and the name is beginning to be seen on respected labels.

Seyval Blanc: Probably the white hybrid with the most assured future, Seyval makes a dry, light-bodied wine of appealing bouquet and taste. If well made, seyval blanc can compete with some of the classier white wines of the world. One of a few hybrids which needn't be blended to make good wine.

Verdelet Blanc: The vine is fairly vigorous; the grapes are of good eating quality and yield sweet juice. The wine is low in acid; it is a pleasing, slightly fragrant wine which is improved by aging in oak.

Vidal Blanc: A hybrid developed from *ugni blanc* (*trebbiano*, in Italy). Its wine is soft, semi-dry, sometimes has an apple nose.

Villard Blanc: A big producer, it makes a good blending wine of rather neutral character. By itself it produces a naturally semi-sweet white wine.

For Red Wines

Baco Noir: Widely planted, early-ripening, excellent grape of cabernet.

sauvignon derivation. Makes a good "bordeaux type" wine that ages well. It's the dependable red to compare with the dependable white seyval blanc.

Cascade: Extensively planted in the Finger Lakes region of New York, these grapes make a light-colored wine, so are often used for rosé wine or for blending material for wines made of such grapes as *baco noir* and *Maréchal Foch.*

Chambourcin: Thought to have a great future in the Midwest, but not yet widely planted. The vine is hardy, the wine of superior quality, and it improves greatly when aged in oak.

Chancellor: Wine from this grape is French in character. Chancellor is planted widely in France. It makes full-bodied, heavy, deep red wine, forthright, not subtle, and without too much finesse.

Chelois: Pronounced *shelloy* by some winemakers, and *shell-wah* (as the French pronounce it) by others. This productive vine has been well tested in the Midwest and makes good wine of bordeaux character if well aged in oak.

Colobel: A grape with color intensity ten to fifteen times what is usual. It thus makes excellent blending material for color improvement. It is not, nor is it intended to be, a good varietal wine. It is simply a *teinturier*, or color-giver.

De Chaunac: The juice of these grapes is a bit light in color and so makes a good dry rosé, or may be blended with wine of deeper color for red wine.

Florental: A gamay hybrid which may be used to make a beaujolais type of wine. It is not easy to grow.

Foch or *Maréchal Foch:* Of Alsatian origin, the grape makes a high quality wine which ages well. It is often called a burgundy type; it has pinot noir in its heritage.

Millot or *Leon Millot:* Of the same group of hybrids as Foch, it ripens a bit earlier, so may suit some locations better.

Most of the French hybrid grapes make better wine if they are blended. "The varietal situation as regards both red and white hybrids is very fluid and will remain so for a long time," says Philip Wagner. "It takes decades to discover the faults as well as the virtues of a variety. Lots of very promising things are still in the works, and breeding continues."

Native Grapes of the Midwest

For White Wines

Catawba: One of the earliest native grapes used for wine, it is still heavily planted along the Ohio shores of Lake Erie as well as in New York's Finger Lakes district. It has long been used for sparkling wines and is popular as a pink wine, the color being provided by other grapes. It's a good table grape.

Delaware: Best of the native grapes for winemaking, a favorite for sparkling wines, good as a still wine. A pink grape with white juice and a more delicate aroma than other native varieties. Delaware, Ohio, not the state of Delaware, is responsible for the name.

Dutchess: An old American hybrid which makes an agreeable wine. The vine is moderately productive and grows well throughout most of the Midwest. It would be more widely planted but the vine is not vigorous and is subject to fungus diseases. Dutchess grapes are good table grapes.

Niagara: A grape that makes a sweet, golden wine, usually quite foxy. The vine is productive, but this grape isn't going anywhere. Its days are numbered because so many better white wine varieties have come along to replace it.

For Red Wines

Concord: This big juice and jelly grape makes the foxiest wine of all, and while it has its devotees and its juices are useful in some sherries and ports as well as in the once-popular "cold duck," there is evidence that the concord has had its day as a wine grape. It is being replaced all over the Midwest by French-American hybrids, and most new vineyards offer it no space at all. (In 1975 and 1976 the big wineries such as

Taylor Wine Company in New York, drastically reduced their purchases of concord, reportedly because they were getting an uncomfort-
able backlash on foxiness.)

Vinifera: Classic Wine Grapes of the Midwest

For White Wines

Chardonnay: The famous white burgundy grape and champagne grape
of France does exceptionally well in California's northern, cooler vineyards. Here and there in Midwestern protected vineyards it responds to
exceptional care, and produces small crops for limited bottlings of excellent wine.

Gewürztraminer: The famous spicy grape of Alsace has been planted in
a few Midwestern vineyards but hasn't had a chance to prove itself as
yet.

Johannisberg Riesling: The correct name is white riesling, the Johannisberg having been retained to indicate its relationship to the great
German wine grape of the Schloss Johannisberg estate. A few small
Midwestern wineries have had remarkable success with it, but a favorable microclimate and much tender, loving care are required to culti-
vate this vine with success.

Müller-Thurgau: Thought to be a cross of riesling and sylvaner made
by Dr. Müller-Thurgau, a Swiss, at Geisenheim University in the
1880s, the vine is more cold-resistant, thrives on poorer soil, and ripens
earlier than white riesling. The wine is delicate, soft, and fragrant.

For Red Wines

Cabernet Sauvignon: The great red grape of Bordeaux and California
is not expected ever to be a commercial success in cold Midwestern
territory, but here and there some showcase cabernet sauvignon has
been produced, and the growers and winemakers deserve all the ap-

plause they've been getting. The vine is a "shy bearer" even under the best of circumstances.

Gamay, Gamay Beaujolais: The gamay, or gamay noir, grape of California is thought to be the true beaujolais grape, while the gamay beaujolais is now considered to be a clone of the pinot noir. These grapes produce fruity red wines in the West and are planted sketchily in the Midwest, in favorable microclimates.

Pinot Noir: The red Burgundian grape is not expected to be a commercial success in the Midwest, but it is successful in a very small way for a very few wineries. A shy bearer under the best growing conditions, it is now meeting with success in California because of improved technology and more careful site selection.

Ruby Cabernet: A cross between cabernet sauvignon and carignane, developed at the University of California, Davis, for better adaptation to both very warm and very cool climates, the ruby cabernet makes a pleasant, medium-bodied red wine. It hasn't proved itself yet in Midwestern vineyards.

It should be kept in mind that a grape's membership in the **vinifera** family is not in itself a pedigree. While it is true that all of the world's great wines at present are made from vinifera grapes, it is also true that most of the world's *vin ordinaire* is likewise made of grapes belonging to that family. The Thompson seedless grape is as much a vinifera as the chardonnay.

Too much emphasis on the fancied potential of vinifera in the cold climate of the Midwest and East can mislead winegrowers into some costly errors. Not much publicity has been given to the failures. For example, in the spring of 1977 a Hudson River Valley vineyard pulled out 1,500 cabernet sauvignon and 1,200 chardonnay vines because of drastic winter-kill and no production. They were replaced with French hybrids. Vinifera grape varieties also suffered badly in New York in late 1980.

Lynfred Winery

PRIVATE RESERVE

MICHIGAN
PEACH WINE

BERRIEN COUNTY

BOTTLE NUMBER_____OF _3580_

Produced And Bottled By
Lynfred Winery • Roselle, Illinois
Bonded Winery No. 33 Alcohol 10.8% By Volume

The Wines
of Illinois

The land of Lincoln is known for its corn, hogs and soybeans, not for its grapes. But there is hope that small wineries may come into existence within the next few years, as they did in Indiana when repressive Prohibition-era laws were revoked. There is a history of wine growing in Illinois, along the Mississippi. Surely it can be revived with the help of favorable legislation enacted in 1981.

Nauvoo, on the Mississippi in southern Illinois, has a fascinating and unique history that blends Mormonism, communism, French influences, wine, and cheese. Today the "wedding of wine and cheese" is still celebrated in Nauvoo on the weekend prior to the Labor Day weekend.

Nauvoo is a mecca for members of the Church of the Latter Day Saints who come to see the restored Mormon homes, including those of Joseph Smith and Brigham Young. Nauvoo itself was founded by Joseph Smith and was a Mormon settlement from 1839 to 1846. After being persecuted and driven out of Nauvoo, the Mormons began their long trek to Utah under the leadership of Brigham Young. But not before Joseph Smith and his brother Hyrum had been shot and killed while in the "protective custody" of the Carthage, Illinois, jail.

The Mormons were followed by French Icarian communists who were not successful in establishing their brand of communism, but who stayed long enough to plant vineyards and carve wine caves along the river. They are said to have tended at least 800 acres of grapes. Some of their vines remain as an historical curiosity, and many old wine tunnels remain. But the only surviving winery is that of the Baxter family, the Gem City Vineland Company.

A cheerful note may be added here. Until very recently, it was illegal in Illinois for a winery to sell, or even offer samples of its products on the premises. While one could visit the Baxters, their wines could not be tasted. Now visitors may taste and buy at the winery. In the past, such repressive laws have discouraged the development of small wineries in the Midwest, but now it's possible that viticulture may be reestablished on the banks of the Mississippi, and that the honeycomb of wine tunnels on the river's banks (those not needed for Nauvoo's famous cheese) can be restored to their intended use.

Elsewhere in Illinois, there have been other kinds of problems. In a corn-growing state, nobody worries about the welfare of grapes except those who want to grow them. Herbicides used for corn crops did in the first winery established at Monee by Bernard Ramey and his partner, the late Joseph Allen. John Thompson, Ramey and Allen's successor, having won the cooperation of his neighbor farmers, is having more success.

There's promise for the future of Illinois farm wineries in Terra Vineyards, owned by Wilfred and Linda Enders of Port Byron, a small Mississippi River town above Moline. The couple purchased 5,000 French hybrid cuttings from the Wollersheim Winery (Wisconsin) in the spring of 1976, and followed the next year with 1,500 grafted vinifera vines from Hermann Wiemer, the well-known German grower and winemaker of New York's Finger Lakes district.

With good fortune and hard work, the Enderses will have chardonnay, riesling, sauvignon blanc and merlot, along with baco, foch, millot and seyval to make wines for their 10,000 gallon winery.

Gem City Vineland Company, Inc.

ESTABLISHED 1857

So. Parley St., Nauvoo, IL 62354

Phone: 217-453-2218

President, Hilde F. Baxter; vice-president, Dorothy O. Baxter; vine-yard manager, Fred Baxter.

Vineyard: 30 acres delaware and concord. They also buy from growers.

Visiting: April to October. Cassette-guided tours daily 7:00 a.m.-5:00 p.m. Saturday, 10:00 a.m.-5:00 p.m. Sunday 12:00-5:00 p.m.

Storage capacity: 40,000 gallons.

Directions: From Chicago area, I-80 west to I-74, (south) to Galesburg, U.S. 34 west to U.S. 96, south to Nauvoo on the Mississippi River. Watch for signs.

The Baxters' winery was not the earliest in Nauvoo. The first vintner was a Swiss, John Tanner, who planted grapes in 1847. Alois Rheinberger, from Lichtenstein, who founded a winery in 1850, is well remembered in Nauvoo because his winery is now the city's historical museum, and because, behind the museum, there remains an acre of vines he planted. They still bear grapes, and are a part of the city's historical treasure.

Emil Baxter, though English, came to Nauvoo with the Icarians, who were led by Etienne Cabet, a writer, historian of the French Revolution, and former attorney-general and deputy of France. Baxter was secretary of the colony. When it disbanded after two years and its members scattered, Baxter remained with his winery. Fred Baxter is the fifth generation owner.

The Baxters have been growing concord and delaware grapes while buying other native grapes from growers to sell as fresh fruit in Chicago, Minneapolis, and other markets. Now that restrictions on selling wine at the winery have been removed, you can sample their wine, and they let you sample Nauvoo blue cheese with it.

The Baxter wine is an important part of the annual festival at Nauvoo when the wedding of wine and cheese is depicted. It is part of the pageant "Quashquema* to Nauvoo." In the ceremony celebrated only in Roquefort, France and Nauvoo, Illinois, the "bride" places wine on a barrel, the "groom" places cheese, and the "magistrate" weds the two, cheese and wine, by encircling them with a barrel hoop.

Other activities at the time include parades, floats, races, group ka-

---

* Old Indian name for Nauvoo.

rate, band music, and a beer fest. Every year, as many as fifteen-thousand people come to this historic, charming Mississippi town for the wedding of wine and cheese.

Wines of Gem City Vineland

WHITE WINE

Niagara, sweet.
Sauterne, dry.

RED WINE

Burgundy, dry.
Concord, sweet.
Rosé, medium sweet.

All wines are Old Nauvoo brand, available also in jugs.
Price of wines: About $2.85.

Lynfred Winery

ESTABLISHED 1975

15 South Roselle Road, Roselle, IL 60172

Phone: 312-529-1000

Owner, president, Fred E. Koehler; secretary-treasurer, co-winemaker, Lynn Star Taylor (Mrs. Fred E. Koehler).

Vineyard: 1 acre. Most fruit and juices purchased from California and Michigan.

Visiting: Wednesday through Sunday, noon-8:00 p.m. Closed January.

Storage capacity: 10,000 gallons.

Directions: From Chicago, west past O'Hare Airport on Irving Park Road, through Bensonville, Wooddale, Itasca to Roselle Road. Left, (south) about 1 block, first house on left is winery.

Fred Koehler is general manager of the Itasca Country Club, and Lynn was catering manager, until their winemaking hobby got the better of them. Koehler's father and grandfather were winemakers, so the involvement with wine came naturally. The Koehlers' daughter, Diane, helps in the winemaking and winery activities.

The winery is a large house built in 1912, on land that earlier belonged to Col. Roselle M. Hough, for whom the town of Roselle was named. He sold the property to the Hattendorf family, who owned the local lumber yard, and they built the house for their daughter's wedding present. The Koehlers have restored it with stained glass windows adding charm to the tasting room. Visitors may see all processes in winemaking.

Lynn, who is creative, works with wood as well as food and wine. She carved the image of the winery for an identifying sign to be placed in front. The Koehlers do not plan to expand the vineyard, where they grow baco noir and vidal blanc grapes.

Wines of Lynfred Winery

Fruit wines include montmorency and bing cherry wines, red currant, pear, peach, plum and strawberry.

WHITE WINE

Malaga (California grapes).
Vidal Blanc (from Michigan).

RED WINE

Baco Noir
Concord
California wines from alicante bouschet, barbera, cabernet sauvignon, carignane, mataro, and zinfandel grapes.

Price of wines: $5.00 to $7.00; Cabernet, $11.00.

Thompson Winery

ESTABLISHED 1964

P.O. Box 127, Monee, IL 60449
Phone: 312-534-8050

President and general manager, John E. Thompson; cellarmaster, Joe Marcukaitis.

Vineyard: 30 acres delaware, French hybrids.

Visiting: Tours Sundays 1:00 p.m.-4:00 p.m. From May through September, also Saturdays 1:00 p.m.-4:00 p.m.

Storage capacity: 18,500 gallons.

Directions: From Chicago, Dan Ryan Expressway into Highway 57. Off at Monee to Rt. 50. South of Monee about 1½ miles on 50 to Pauling Road overpass; west to winery on hilltop.

John Thompson is a man of many interests. One of the most visible is his hobby of collecting steam trains. He has parked one of them at the winery along with an ancient steam tractor. Several cars behind the steam locomotive are used for wine storage. One is a guest house, and another, the dining car, is used for special luncheons, which Thompson prepares himself. He's a good cook, not surprisingly, since for many years he has been a meat packer and food processor. Thompson recently sold the food business in order to give more time to the winery, but he still owns several thousand acres of rich Illinois farmland (Thompson Farms) where he fattens 3,000 head of beef cattle a year.

Thompson also teaches wine appreciation classes in the adult education program of a neighboring high school and to home economics students at Prairie State College in Chicago Heights.

In Portugal, they speak of giving wine its "education" in the lodges of the big port shippers. Thompson's sparkling wines (*méthode champenoise*) should be well educated if they emulate their owner, a man with B.A., M.B.A., M.S., and Ph.D. degrees from the Illinois Institute of Technology and the University of Chicago.

A collector of trains would have a natural interest in a defunct winery comprised of two old Illinois Central train stations. The problem was that Bernard Ramey's Ramey and Allen Winery was put out of business by the floating poisons of weed killers intended for fields of Illinois corn. They shriveled the grapes. But Thompson persuaded his neighbors to use other herbicides, of the non-volatile kind, and has restored the vineyards since he bought the winery in 1969.

He makes only sparkling wines, but plays with delightful ideas such as making a sparkling zinfandel of California grapes. A little zinfandel is used to make his Cuvée Père Hennepin pink.

Thompson is fascinated by the tales of the early French Jesuit missionary explorers "who first made wine here and sought to bring peace and brotherhood to the wilderness." The Père label was chosen because Père Marquette passed the winter of 1674 at the site of the winery, after his famous voyage with Louis Jolliet.

Wines of Thompson Winery

Père Champagne
Cuvée Père Marquette, Brut and Extra Dry.
Père Champagne
Cuvée Père Hennepin, made pink with zinfandel.

Price of wines: About $6.00.

The Wines of Indiana

In 1802, Congress granted to Jean Jacques Dufour and his band of Swiss countrymen the right to plant 2,500 acres of grape vines in what is now Switzerland County, Indiana. Dufour had previously made unsuccessful attempts to grow grapes across the Ohio River in the young state of Kentucky. Some historians say that it was Ben Franklin who invited Dufour to come to the new country and make wine. It is said that Franklin sympathized with French soldiers who missed their customary daily wines while serving in the American Revolution. Franklin himself loved wine. "Wine is a constant proof that God loves us and loves to see us happy," he said.

Those first Indiana grape growers tended their plantings so well that a successful commercial winery was established, which thrived until the late 1820's. Then black rot despoiled the vineyards, and the Swiss settlers turned to other agricultural crops.

It took more than 150 years for grapes and wine to return to Indiana. Two of the men who brought them back were Professor William Oliver of the University of Indiana, and Ben Sparks, a retired commander of the U.S. Navy.

While law professor Oliver was working out the legal angles of establishing small wineries in the state of Indiana, Ben Sparks was attacking the bastions of temperance still lingering in the state. He was successful in persuading Purdue University and its agricultural extension specialists to help him sponsor an annual grape-wine symposium, and he lobbied successfully for the establishment of the Indiana Winegrowers Guild.

Both Oliver and Sparks now operate their own wineries with the full partnership of their ladies, Mary and Lee.

A future Indiana winery is Hunt-Burneau Vineyards, established by Gerald and Carolyn Anderson of Greenwich, Connecticut, on the Frankfort farm of Carolyn's mother, Helen Hunt. Mrs. Hunt is an extraordinary woman who grows flowers and vegetables and operates a commercial greenhouse, while teaching Latin and English in Frankfort High School, and composition at the college level two evenings a week. Helen Hunt, the gardener, planted a thousand vines for the Andersons' winery. They are chardonnay, florental, chambourcin, ravat, Foch, and others. The Andersons fly in from Connecticut on frequent weekends to assist with the work and so that Anderson may continue his experimental winemaking in the future commercial winery, which has an air-conditioned cellar. Anderson, the son of Clifford Anderson, former secretary of the Navy, is a former investment banker who now owns a chemical company and has an office in Rockefeller Plaza, New York. Carolyn Anderson is a writer and decorator. She is sure that the vineyard will thrive with her mother's "shadow on the vines."

The Hoosier state lost its earliest 1970's winery, Treaty Line Wine Cellars, but casualties have been very few and Indiana seems well on the way toward recognition as a wine state.

Banholzer Winecellars Ltd.
ESTABLISHED 1974

Rt. 1000 North, New Carlisle, IN 46552

Phone: 219-778-2448

Owners, Carl and Janet Banholzer.

Vineyard: 72 acres vinifera and hybrids.

Picnic area.

Visiting: March-December, 11:00 a.m.-5:00 p.m. Closed Monday,

Tuesday. Tours at 1:00 and 3:00 include wine art gallery. Sight-Sound program at noon, 2:00, and 4:00 p.m. Seated tasting of 6 wines with cheese, $3.00.

Storage capacity: 35,460 gallons.

Directions: From Chicago, 60 miles. I-94 to Michigan, Exit 1, right. One mile back to I-94, left at 1000 North, follow signs, 6 miles.

Cabernet sauvignon from *Indiana*? It was unthinkable in 1975. The Banholzer Cabernet Sauvignon 1975 made an international splash, startling the French publication *Le Monde* into headlines and bringing press and television newswriters and cameras to the Banholzer winery. The wine was excellent and sold for a high price.

Unhappily, three exceptionally poor harvests followed, and not only was there not enough cabernet to sell subsequently, but there was very little wine from the French hybrid vines in those years, and Banholzer Winecellars was near financial collapse. The winery was advertised for sale in early 1980, and the doors were closed. A glum Banholzer, veteran of fifteen years in the business (he was founder of Tabor Hill Vineyards earlier) guessed he "might go back into social service work."

He admitted later, though, that even when the outlook was darkest, he had visions of some "angel" coming to the rescue. And someone did. The winery reopened in the fall with new wines, exciting new plans, and a solid financial base. The rescuer was Arthur Curry of Lehman Bros., Chicago, a member of Banholzer Winecellars Wine Society of several thousand members. Curry and several others came into the organization as limited partner investors. They purchased a chardonnay vineyard and arranged for other grape supplies in California to enable the Banholzers to make wines for the 1980 harvest season with the new vineyard crop and some wines in oak in the cellars. It is expected that several of the future Banholzer wines will carry a bit of California in their blends.

There are grape stomps and Bacchanals and other events again in this handsome winery which is a restored barn more than 100 years old. The future looks bright.

Wines of Banholzer Winecellars
First Indiana Champagne

WHITE WINE

Pinot Chardonnay
La Fleur, a little sweet.
Sweet Harvest May Wine

RED WINE

Cabernet Sauvignon
Kaisertahl, dry.
Nouveau Rouge burgundy, medium dry.
Picnic Rosé, sweet.

Price of Wines: $5.00-$9.00 (champagne).

Easley Enterprises, Inc.
ESTABLISHED 1974

205 N. College Ave., Indianapolis, IN 46202

Phone: 317-636-4516

President and winemaker, John Easley; secretary, Joan Easley.

Vineyard: 120 acres, 50 acres planted.

Visiting: Noon-6:00 p.m. Monday-Saturday. Closed Sundays. Tours for groups of 12 or more (with wine-tasting and cheese).

Storage capacity: 10,000 gallons.

Directions: Take I-65 or I-70 to Indianapolis, Exit 111. The winery is the first property off the downtown ramp. Watch for signs.

John and Joan Easley's Cape Sandy Vineyards are on a four hundred foot bluff jutting into the Ohio River where winds and waters exert a beneficial influence on the grape vines. At harvest time the grapes are rushed the 160 miles to the Indianapolis winery by night and crushed next morning.
   The Easleys became interested in winegrowing when they owned a

summer home in Michigan's fruit belt, where they and their two children spent many happy days. They invested in a Michigan winery first, then developed their Ohio River property some time later.

The Easleys invite those who have visited their tasting room to their May fest and limit the number to 500. They make a May wine to drink and there is simple food. A German band plays and there is singing by the Maennerchor, which John Easley says is the oldest male choir in the world. The choir originated in Indianapolis.

John and Joan do all of the winery work themselves at present. Easley claims to be janitor as well as winemaker.

Wines of Easley's Cape Sandy Vineyards

WHITE WINE

Seyval Blanc, dry.
White Wine, semi-sweet.
Dutchess, dessert wine.

RED WINE

Baco Noir, semi-dry.
Chelois, light, dry.
De Chaunac, semi-dry, heavy-bodied.
Seibel 13053, semi-sweet.
Red, semi-dry, medium body.
Rosé, sweet.

Price of wines: $2.75-$3.10.

Golden Rain Tree Winery, Inc.
ESTABLISHED 1974

RR 2, Wadesville, IN 47638

Phone: 812-963-6441

President: Robert Hahn; vice-president, enologist, Murli Dharmadhikari.

Vineyards: About 3 acres. Grapes purchased from local growers.

Restaurant.

Visiting: Tuesday-Thursday, 11:00 a.m.-10:00 p.m. Friday, Saturday to midnight. Sunday, to 8:00 p.m. Tours: 11:00 a.m., 2:00 p.m., and 4:00 p.m.; until 7:00 p.m. for special parties, by appointment.

Storage capacity: 50,000 gallons.

Directions: From East-West I-64 to 65 south toward Evansville. Off at Boonville, New Harmony Road. Follow signs for St. Wendel and Golden Rain Tree Winery, about 2 miles.

Two horticulturists operate Rain Tree. Albert Weil grows peaches and apples as well as grapes; Murli Dharmadhikari, who is from India, holds a doctorate in horticulture from Ohio State University. These experts advise local farmers how to grow the grapes they need for winemaking, and purchase the produce from thirty acres. Their chief interest is in French hybrid varieties. Weil has planted a few acres of seyval blanc, villard blanc, baco noir, and de Chaunac.

The winery is a Swiss-German chalet built on a basic A-frame with a deck around the outside so that in summer when there are special parties, people may sip their wine out-of-doors. Inside, the tasting room (over the cellar) is equipped with heavy wooden furniture in German style. The walls are of barn wood, and there is a fireplace to make the tasting room a welcoming, friendly place in cool weather. There is live music on weekends and a wine fest at harvest time.

Golden Rain Tree Criterion white wine tied for top honors with a Markko Riesling in Wineries Unlimited 1980 Eastern Competition.

Golden Rain Tree Winery was named for the Oriental trees that have grown along streets and in gardens and parks of Posey County since they were introduced in 1828. In summer, they rain golden blossoms.

Wines of Golden Rain Tree Winery

WHITE WINE

Apple and peach wines
Chablis, villard blanc.
Criterion White, vidal blend.
Shanti, seyval blend.
St. Wendel White, niagara blend.

RED WINE

Burgundy, chelois and Foch.
St. Wendel Red, concord blend.
Rosé, aurora and baco.
St. Wendel Rosé, catawba blend.
Director's Choice, chelois blend.
Criterion Red, hybrid blend.
Spirit of '76, concord, catawba baco blend.

Price of wines: $3.50-$4.50.

Huber Orchard Winery
ESTABLISHED 1978

Route 1, Box 202, Borden IN 47106

Phone: 812-923-WINE

Partners, Carl and Gerald Huber.

Vineyards: 15 acres; 90 acres apple orchards.

Visiting: June-October, 10:00 a.m.-8:00 p.m. daily. Saturday till 11:00 p.m.; Sunday 10:00 a.m.-6:00 p.m. Other months, somewhat shorter hours except Saturday. No Sunday sales. Closed Sunday January-May.

Storage capacity: 50,000 gallons.

Directions: From Louisville, Kentucky: I-64 west 4 miles to Galena exit. Turn north at Galena on Navilleton Road 6 miles. Blue and white signs will guide you.

The Huber brothers and their families live on the ancestral farm that, for six generations, was a dairy farm. Their father sold his cows when World War II came along and all his help was drafted. Carl and Gerald turned the apple orchards into a "you pick" operation, and from there, since the brothers had been making wines as amateurs for nineteen years, the transition to a winery was easy.

There was the huge, 150-year-old dairy barn. Said Gerald, in his southern Indiana drawl, "It was just laying there crying." That barn is happy now that it has become a winery, and the Huber brothers have also built an underground cellar for aging and storing their wines.

Their vineyards are experimental. "We are going to see what will grow and then plant those grapes with the help of our sons," says Gerald Huber. Each partner has four children, seven boys and one girl in all. When the older boys finish high school, they'll join their fathers in the family business of winegrowing. Native and hybrid grapes but no vinifera are growing on the Huber farm, and the brothers have been buying as many as thirteen varieties of grapes for their winemaking. They are good friends of the Schuchters of Valley Vineyards in Ohio, and acknowledge the assistance and advice of others, particularly Bill Oliver, who, declares Gerald, "must be the granddaddy of all the Indiana winegrowers."

"It's a fascinating business, but it takes a ton of money," Huber sighs. To which all other winegrowers would say, "Amen."

Wines of Huber Orchard Winery

Apple and strawberry fruit wines, from farm crops. Sparkling niagara (non alcoholic).

WHITE WINE

Aurora
Seyval Blanc
Vidal Blanc
Niagara
Starlite White

RED WINE

Baco Noir
Catawba Rosé
Chancellor
Chelois
De Chaunac
Concord
St. John's Red

Price of wines: $3.25-$6.00.

Oliver Wine Company, Inc.

ESTABLISHED 1972

8024 North Highway 37, Bloomington, IN 47401

Phone: 812-876-5800

Owners, William and Mary Oliver; enologist and plant manager, John Hartman.

Vineyard: 24 acres now in production.

Visiting: Daily 11:00 a.m.-6:00 p.m. Closed Sundays.

Storage capacity: 24,000 gallons.

Directions: Highway 37 to Bloomington; 6 to 7 miles north of Bloomington on east side of road. Watch for signs.

William W. Oliver, professor of law at Indiana University in Bloomington, drafted the Indiana Small Wineries Act of 1971 and prodded it through the legislature without a flap. Ask him how he accomplished that, in a state where wine had been equated with drunkenness (not that people didn't *drink*, you understand!), and Oliver chuckles:
"It's easy when so many legislators are your former students!"
Bill and Mary Oliver were among the first to open a small winery in Indiana. Their attractive tasting room is close to the highway and passing traffic. It is a popular spot with students, who come mostly for Camelot Mead, the Oliver honey wine. A hot-air balloon piloted by the Olivers' son, Bill, has advertised Camelot Mead since 1976, when Bill, at sixteen, was the youngest pilot of hot-air balloons in the country.
Nearby is the greenhouse, where Oliver grows vines by mist propagation, which he sells to others or plants in his own vineyards. Varieties available include aurora, baco, cascade, foch, seyval blanc, vidal, and villard noir.
The tasting room sells cheese and T-shirts and other knick-knacks. Mary Oliver presides there, for the law professor-vineyard man leads a double life—even a triple life. Oliver is the man who persuaded the Falcon Coal Company of Kentucky to restore the beauty of stripmined mountain land by planting vineyards (which he supervises).

The Olivers built their winery with royalties from Oliver's writing in the field of federal taxation and with his consultant's fees.

The annual wine and music festival at the winery draws as many as 14,000 visitors.

Wines of Oliver Winery

WHITE WINE

Aurora
Camelot Mead, honey wine.
Country White, aurora and villard blanc.
Seyval Blanc

RED WINE

Baco Noir
Cascade
Country Red, baco and chelois.
De Chaunac
Big Red, sweet.
Indiana Red
Millot
Rosé de Chaunac

Price of wines: $3.25-$5.00.

Possum Trot Vineyards
ESTABLISHED 1978

8310 North Possum Trot Road, Unionville, IN 47468

Phone: 812-988-2694

Owners, Ben and Leora Sparks.

Vineyards: 5 acres.

Visiting: 9:00 a.m.-6 p.m. daily except Sunday.

Storage capacity: 1500 gallons.

Directions: From Indianapolis, take Route 135 south to Bean Blossom, west on state 45 to Trevlac. Immediately after Trevlac sign, turn right over railroad tracks, then turn left. Check your odometer and drive 2.1 miles to Possum Trot Road. Go right 1/3 mile to first house on the right. Watch for a guiding sign at the railroad.

The approach is on a narrow, winding road; it is hilly, woodsy and rural along the northern shore of Lake Lemon, where Ben and Lee Sparks live, grow grapes and welcome you to their winery. It is a less plush life than the Sparkses led when Ben was a Naval commander, but you have only to be greeted by these two warm and friendly people to know that they aren't missing much. Ben is a native Hoosier.

All the travel (he was an aviator with over 8,000 hours of flight time) while in the service helped Ben develop a taste for good wine, and his retirement threatened to cut down the supply. So, the Sparks family found an old farmhouse in beautiful Brown County, Indiana, and moved in 1968, when January winds were howling. Three of the four Sparks sons were still with their parents, and helped cut wood to stoke the fires of the wood-burning stove which heated the entire house. There was no indoor plumbing. "Once warmed, we tackled the problem of modernizing the house," recalls Ben.

Very soon, he started planting grapes. He scratched all vinifera after losing overnight a cabernet-riesling vineyard in its second year. The thermometer had suddenly dipped from a balmy sixty degrees to a wild twenty-five below zero. Sparks found no help at Purdue, so he became his own viticultural experiment station and found that baco noir, de Chaunac, chancellor, and Foch were his best grapes for red wines, while aurora, vidal blanc, seyval blanc, and cayuga were his best white wine grapes.

Ben wasn't a Navy officer for nothing. He took to prodding the people at Purdue and finally got them to help him sponsor a grape-wine symposium, which became an annual event and aroused great enthusiasm, not only from the university, but among others who wanted to grow grapes and make wine.

Meanwhile, Bill Oliver was prodding the legislature to make it possible for small wineries to exist. The Olivers, and Oliver Winery, are not too far from Possum Trot. The two couples are good friends.

When Possum Trot Winery opened in 1978, Ben and Lee were ready.

Behind them lay a great deal of work, planning, and experimentation. At present, they sell just two wines, a white and a red.

Wines of Possum Trot Vineyards

WHITE WINE

Light Wine (Vignoles or Vidal).

RED WINE

Foch

Price of Wines: $4.00.

Rauner and Sons
ESTABLISHED 1977

314 Dixieway North (U.S. 31), South Bend, IN 46637

Phone: 219-277-4078

Owner, general manager, winemaker, James Rauner; secretary, Peter Rauner; sales manager, Paul Rauner; vineyard manager, John Rauner; winemaker, Joe Rauner; chemist, Margaret Kastner.

Vineyards: Small experimental vineyard, most grapes purchased. Winemaking and beermaking equipment, wine accessories, and books; wines of California and Europe available.

Visiting: Monday through Saturday, 11:00 a.m.-6:00 p.m. all year. Closed Sunday.

Storage capacity: 6,000 gallons.

Directions: South Bend exit from I-80-90, Cleveland Road. North on Dixie Highway (U.S. 31) about 3/4 mile. Look for Wine World sign, on right.

James Rauner, an ordained deacon in the Catholic Church, teaches theology in St. Joseph's High School in South Bend. The Rauners, parents of nine children, were enthusiastic amateur winemakers and are friends of several winemaking families. So, it seemed very natural to them to turn to commercial winemaking as a family project. The oldest four of the five Rauner sons have been given important responsibilities in the winery management, though until school days are over, they can work only part-time. The same is true of their father.

When you phone Rauner and Sons, a cheerful voice greets you: "Wine World!" If you call when the winery is closed, a recorded message tells you what's going on at the winery and wishes you a happy weekend.

Wines of Rauner and Sons

Apple wine, sangria

WHITE WINE

Chablis
Niagara
Sauterne

RED WINE

Baco Noir
Burgundy
Premium Claret
Maréchal Foch
Rosé (dry, medium, and sweet).

Price of wines: $2.95-$3.95.

Swiss Valley Vineyards
ESTABLISHED 1974

101 Ferry St., Vevay, IN 47043

Phone: 812-427-2201 (winery); 513-521-5096 (residence)

Owner and operator, Albert F. Meyer.

Vineyard: 3 acres. Some grapes purchased from growers.

Visiting: Winter months, Friday and Saturday 9:00 a.m.-9:00 p.m. Starting in June, Wednesday-Saturday 9:00 a.m.-9:00 p.m.

Storage capacity: 1,000 gallons.

Directions: From Indianapolis, I-74 to Cincinnati, down 156 to Vevay. At the only flashing light in town, go south to the river. It is on Ferry St. near the ferry.

Alvin and Margaret Meyer and their 11 children, of Cincinnati, enjoyed camping at Vevay and attending the annual festival there for a number of years. While it was always called a *wine* festival, there was no wine, and the Meyer family thought that very curious.

"There weren't even any grapes!" exclaimed Marge Meyer.* "We talked about it, went to the library and studied the history of the place, and then said to ourselves, '*We* will plant grapes here!' " And that's how wine-growing was re-established in Switzerland County, Indiana.

It was lucky for Vevay and its annual festival that the Meyer family became interested, for once the Meyer family gets involved in a project, they really work at it. Seven of the younger generation of Meyers are married and even their spouses are workers in this new winery. All of them live and many work in Cincinnati, but the distance is only a few miles and there's a four-room house in Vevay, as well as another tiny house on the vineyard site to help accommodate this big family of grape-growers and wine enthusiasts. Before they had any grapes of their own, they made wine from juices procured from other wineries.

Swiss Valley Vineyards have their own two-day Swiss Valley Winery Festival in July, in connection with the summer-long town festival. It includes grape-stomping, stone-tossing, German music, and of course, Meyer's wines. In town, there are turtle races, performances of "The Hoosier Boy," and a "Patchwork Festival," which includes not only quilts, but other crafts as well.

When you visit this beautiful, historical wine-growing site on the Ohio River, it's very likely that you'll run into at least one Meyer. If you're lucky, you may meet a dozen!

Wines of Swiss Valley Vineyards

Apple
Concord
Red (blend of hybrids).
Rosé

Price of wines: About $3.00.

---

* The death of Mrs. Meyer temporarily inactivated this winery in 1979. "It hurts too much," Alvin said. "But we are going new ways, meeting new friends. We are banking on the town coming alive in tune with its history and the times. We're acquiring more land and plan to open a restaurant."

Villa Medeo Vineyards Winery
ESTABLISHED 1974

Dugan Hollow Rd., RR 2, Madison, IN 47250

Phone: 812-265-2194

Owner, Elizabeth Mancuso.

Vineyard: 13 acres.

Home winemaking supplies.

Visiting: Monday-Friday 11:00 a.m.-4:00 p.m. Saturday 11:00 a.m.-5:00 p.m. Closed Sunday. Tours, private parties by arrangement.

Storage capacity: 15,000 gallons.

Directions: Located 1½ miles from downtown Madison, ¼ mile east of US 421 on Aulenbach Avenue.

The Delta Queen Riverboat stops at Madison, Indiana, on the Ohio River, thirteen times in a summer. To the Mancusos—Liz, and daughter Nancy—that means thirteen visits of three or four hundred people, a large number for a small winery to accommodate at once.

Their "Villa Medeo Wine Cafe" often functions as a neighborhood gathering place when not filled with tourists who sample the wines, buy little loaves of Liz's homemade bread ($1.25 each), some cheese and sit at tables inside, or wander outside to enjoy it. The setting is one of natural beauty—hills, trees, and the big river rolling by. On the hill in back of the winery there's an ancient cave entrance. It is said that during the years of early exploration, a band of Indians would attack travelers on the river then disappear into the cave.

Nancy Mancuso works for a manufacturing company and moonlights with the local veterinary hospital, as she loves animals even more than she loves grapes. Horses are favorites, and the Mancusos own two large sheepdogs and sundry cats.

Picnicking along "Vineyard Creek," barrel races, and a demonstration of making barrels by a cooper are part of Grape Arbor Days at Villa Medeo.

Other tourist attractions in the vicinity are historic homes of architectural significance, Fourth of July Governor's Cup hydroplane races, the annual Muzzleloaders' Shoot at nearby Friendship, and Clifty Falls State Park.

Wines of Villa Medeo

WHITE WINE

Bianca alla Bianca, medium dry (best seller).
May Wine, medium sweet.
Seyval, dry 100 percent varietal.
Vidal, dry 100 percent varietal.
Villa White, semi-sweet labrusca.

RED WINE

Baco, dry 100 percent varietal.
De Chaunac, dry 100 percent varietal.
Robusto Rosso, dry, tart, 3 years in oak.
Villa Red, semi-sweet labrusca.
Villa Rosé, semi-sweet.

Price of wines: $4.00.

The Wines of Iowa

To judge by their third-from-last place on the list of states as wine consumers, Iowans know little about the delights of fermented grape juice. Only the residents of Kentucky and West Virginia drink less wine. However, that picture could change somewhat; there are a dozen wineries in Iowa, though most of them make more rhubarb wine than grape. Most of the grapes they do use are imported from California, Missouri or Michigan.

The corn and soybean state isn't much interested in viticulture, although a grape-wine tradition once existed in the Council Bluffs area and could possibly be revived or encouraged in the Mississippi River Valley on Iowa's eastern border.

It is possible that Iowa's rich, loamy soil is the wrong food for grape vines, and is so precious for corn cultivation that it shouldn't be used for experimental crops.

It is also evident that Iowa grapes, like Illinois grapes, can be ruined by weed-killers commonly used for corn.

All of Iowa's small wineries are interesting to visit, and one is unique.

It is, of all things, a *milk* winery, located in downtown Waukon. Winemaker Phil Weighner tells us that research has been going on for a dozen years, and that commercial milk wine may be available soon. It is straw-colored, dry and nutty in taste, heavier in body and higher in protein than grape wine.

R. A. Collins is president of The Waukon Corporation. Visitors are welcome. Phone 319-568-3401 if you'd like to have a look.

Seven wineries are clustered in the seven villages of the famous Amana Colonies, and there's one at Williamsburg, about ten miles south of South Amana. These wineries, of 8,000-40,000 gallon capacities, sell their wines from the premises where they are made, but can't sell in state liquor stores because of their excess sugar (more than the legal standard), and their classification as homemade wines. The Colonies are famous for their piestengel, or rhubarb wine, and they make other fruit wines. Some also make grape wines, but only one of the Amana Colony wineries owns any vineyards.

These wineries are located in villages within two to five miles of one another, because when the Amanas were settled, back in 1854, that was enough distance to place between groups of religious refugees from Germany, Switzerland, and Alsace who were seeking communal life in a new country. The communal lifestyle lasted for three generations and then, in 1932, the colonists voted to separate religion from earning the daily bread. The communal kitchen gave way to the bakery and meat smoking plant, the winery, and the brewery which were now independently operated. Early skills have been passed to succeeding generations, so that there are still furniture factories in the Amana Colonies where traditional walnut and cherrywood furniture is made and there's still a woolen mill.

The giant Amana Refrigeration Company sends thousands of refrigerators, air conditioners, and microwave ovens to a world market, helping to spread the fame of these villages. Not far to the east is West Branch, Iowa, President Herbert Hoover's birthplace and the location of his presidential library. Visitors from the East may easily stop on the way to the Amana Colonies.

The seven villages are named Homestead, Amana, East Amana, Middle Amana, High Amana, West Amana, and South Amana, no doubt making plenty of trouble for postal authorities. The biblical meaning of Amana is "remain faithful."

Wineries of the Amana Colonies

To arrange for group tours of all 7 villages, write P.O. Box 121, Amana IA 52203, or phone 319-622-3269.

Directions: The colonies are 10 miles north of I-80. From the west, exit at Marengo; from the east, exit at Iowa City and take U.S. 60.

Ackerman Winery, Inc. (1956)

South Amana, IA 52234

Phone: 319-622-3379

President, Leslie J. Ackerman; vice-president, Linda Ackerman.

Wines: Apple, apricot, blackberry, blueberry, cranberry, elderberry, strawberry, plum, rhubarb, dandelion; also concord and catawba from Missouri and Illinois grapes.

Hours: Monday through Saturday, 9:00 a.m.-5:00 p.m. Open one hour later in summer.

Storage capacity: 15,000 gallons.

Price of wines: Around $2.50-$4.00 (elderberry).

Colony Village Winery (1977)

(In the basement of Colony Village Restaurant)

Williamsburg, IA 52361

Phone: 319-622-3379

Owners: Leslie Ackerman, Les Roemig.

Wines: Apricot, apple, "dry grape," rosé (concord and hybrid), blueberry, blackberry, elderberry, cranberry, mulberry, strawberry, montmorency cherry, bing cherry, plum, dandelion.

Hours: 9:00 a.m.-6:00 p.m. daily. Sunday noon-6:00 p.m. in summer (June 1-October).

Tasting Room.

Storage capacity: 10,000 gallons.

Price of wines: About $2.50.

Ehrle Bros. Inc. (1934)

Homestead, IA 52236

Phone: 319-622-3241

President, Arthur Miller; vice-president, Lynda Miller; sales manager, Alma C. Ehrle.

Wines: Rhubarb, strawberry, native grape wines.

Hours: Summer, 9:00 a.m.-8:00 p.m. Winter, 10:00 a.m.-6:00 p.m. Closed Sunday.

Tasting room.

Storage capacity: 6,000 gallons.

Price of wines: $3.00.

Little Amana Winery, Inc. (1971)
Der Weinkeller (1973)

Box 172 A, Amana, IA 52203.

Phone, Little Amana, 319-668-1011; Der Weinkeller, 319-622-3630.

Manager, both shops, Ken Schaefer.

Wines: Blackberry, red and black cherry, cranberry, dandelion, elderberry, dry, medium, and sweet grape wine, dry and sweet rhubarb, strawberry, plum.

Hours: Little Amana, 9:00 a.m.-8:00 p.m. daily, noon-6:00 p.m. Sunday. Der Weinkeller, 9:00 a.m.-6:00 p.m. Closed Sunday.

Price of wines: $3.75.

They share the address as well as ownership and sell the same kinds of wine (made on the separate premises, by law), in spite of the fact that Little Amana and Der Weinkeller are separated by eight miles. Little Amana is part of the Amana Colonies shopping complex on Interstate 80, south of the town of Amana. Der Weinkeller is in town. If you aren't in a hurry, the town of Amana, as well as the wineshop, is worth your while. But if you are speeding along the interstate to some other destination, you can save time by visiting the complex. Little Amana Winery sells glassware and gifts along with wine. Other shops in the complex offer tempting handicrafts, blankets, sweaters, woolen fabrics from the mill, Amana foods and antiques. Just don't be in too much of a hurry, or you may be sorry later!

Old Style Colony Winery, Inc. (1949)

Third St., Middle Amana, IA 52207

Phone: 319-622-3451

Owners, George and Helen Kraus.

Wines: Beet, wild blackberry, red clover, cherry, dandelion, grape (3 kinds), piestengel (rhubarb).

Hours: Daily 10:00 a.m.-6:00 p.m. Closed Sunday.

Tasting room.

Storage capacity: 10,000 gallons.

Price of wines: About $2.40-$4.75.

Old Wine Cellar Winery (1962)

Amana, IA 52203

Phone: 319-622-3116

Owner-Winemaker, Ramon F. Goerler.

Vineyards: 10 acres.

Wines: Dandelion, cherry, white grape, sweet and dry concord, piestengel (rhubarb).
Hours: 10:00 a.m.-6:00 p.m. daily; Sunday, noon-5:00 p.m. Cheese House next door open same hours.

Gift shop.

Storage capacity: 15,000 gallons.

Price of wines: $2.75 to $3.95.

Colony Wines, Inc. (1975)

Amana, IA 52203

Phone: 319-668-2712

President and winemaker, Ramon F. Goerler; secretary-treasurer, Betty J. Goerler.

Wines: Same as those of Old Wine Cellar Winery, plus apple, crabapple, strawberry.

Hours: Summer, 7:30 a.m.-9:30 p.m. After Labor Day, 8:00 a.m.-7:00 p.m.

Storage capacity: 40,000 gallons.

Price of wines: $2.75-$3.95.

Sandstone Winery, Inc. (1960)

Box 7, Amana, IA 52203

Phone: 319-622-3081

President, Elsie Mattes; vice-president, Joseph Mattes.

Wines: Piestengel (rhubarb), cherry, plum, grape.

Hours: 9:00 a.m. to 8:00 p.m. No tours, but if fruit is being processed, visitors may watch.

Storage capacity: 8,000 gallons.

Price of wines: $2.60-$3.60 (sweet cherry).

Village Winery (1973)

Amana, IA 52203

Phone: 319-622-3448

Partners, Don and Eunice Krauss.

Wines: Crabapple, apricot, cranberry, dandelion, elderberry, raspberry, strawberry, cherry, piestengel (rhubarb), grape.

Hours: Summer, 9:00 a.m.-6:00 p.m.; winter, 10:00 a.m.-5:00 p.m. Closed Sunday.

Storage capacity: 15,000 gallons.

Price of wines: $2.75-$3.75.

Christina Wine Cellars
ESTABLISHED 1974

123 A. St., McGregor, IA 52157

Phone: 319-873-3321

Owner, Robert K. Lawlor; enologist and winemaker, Christine K. Lawlor.

Vineyards: None. Grapes and fruit are purchased from growers.

Visiting: May through October, 10:00 a.m.-5:00 p.m. Sunday, noon-5:00 p.m. Open Thanksgiving and Christmas.

Gift shop in winery.

Storage capacity: 8,000 gallons.

Directions: Downtown McGregor across from the town square.

The Robert Lawlor family of Cedar Rapids spent sixteen joyous summers at McGregor, houseboating on the Mississippi, and Lawlor wanted to find something permanent in this beautiful city to keep the family together. So he bought an old building that once housed the Diamond Jo Reynolds Steamboat Lines. He thought it would make a fine winery, but a family winemaker was needed.

Son Scott was not enthusiastic, but Christine, who was just finishing her physical education training at St. Catherine's, liked the idea. Diploma in hand, Chris was ready to go to California and take a speedy course in winemaking.

University of California at Davis was less than interested. She got no encouragement from Fresno State, either. "It came time for school to start, so Christine and her mother got into the car and drove to Fresno," Robert Lawlor says. "The immediate reaction was that the school had never had a girl in enology, let alone a farm girl from Iowa who didn't have the prerequisites normally required."

But Chris was not discouraged, and after a few weeks the administration relented and accepted her as a student in the enology department. "She received a lot of help from other students and her professors," Christine's dad reports. "So instead of spending six months, she stayed two years and got her degree in enology."

In the restoration town of McGregor, Chris began making wines in the converted old steamboat-line headquarters. This plan worked so well that Bob Lawlor found another historical site for a second winery, in LaCrosse, Wisconsin. It was opened in late 1979. Chris' parents, as well as her brother Tim, are deeply involved in the family projects.

Wines of Christina Wine Cellars

Apple Wine, from Gays Mills, Wisconsin apples.
Apricot Wine, from Oregon apricots.
Cherry Wine, from Door County, Wisconsin cherries.
Catawba Wine, from Southern Missouri grapes, medium and sweet.
Concord Wine, from Michigan grapes.
Rosé Wine, from California grapes.

Price of wines: $3.00.

Okoboji Winery, Inc.
ESTABLISHED 1977

Highway 71, Okoboji, IA 51355

Phone: 712-332-2674

President, L. A. Becker, Jr.; secretary, Susan Becker.

Vineyards: None. Fruits purchased.

Visiting: May-September, Monday-Wednesday 10:00 a.m.-7:00 p.m.; Thursday-Saturday until 9:00 p.m. Sunday noon-6:00 p.m. Winery is closed January, February, and March. Other times, daily and Sunday hours are noon-6:00 p.m.

Storage capacity: 8,000 gallons.

Directions: On Highway 71 in Okoboji.

Larry Becker has more fun as a winemaker than he did during his eighteen years as a banker. An experienced amateur winemaker, he had a wish to be involved in a commercial venture catering to the thousands of summer visitors to Lake Okoboji. He felt a winery was the right kind of involvement for the Becker family, which includes four children.

Much of the fun centers around the small town's mythical "University of Okoboji" and its activities. There's an annual "homecoming," replete with dancing, games, and a grape stomp. You can't have the same kind of fun stomping cherries or peaches, so the Beckers imported California Thompson seedless grapes for their stomp, and that led them into grape wine as well as the original fruit wines they were making.

Naturally, there's a University of Okoboji label as well as an Okoboji Winery label. You can guess which label the hordes of summer visitors choose. It's the same wine, under either name.

Such nonsense as promoting three football games for the University of Okoboji, all on November 31st, have drawn attention from some rather dignified national publications, including the *Wall Street Journal*. The triple-threat opponents are Iowa University or Iowa State, whichever team wins *that* match, plus Notre Dame and Nebraska. The University of Okoboji naturally wins all three games on a date the calendar doesn't mention!

Wines of Okoboji Winery

Semi-sweet fruit wines, including apple, cherry, purple plum, peach. Thompson seedless grape wine.

Price of wines: Around $4.00.

Private Stock Winery
ESTABLISHED 1977

926 Eighth Street, Boone, IA 50036

Phone: 515-432-8348

Owners, Thomas H. and Rose Larson.

Vineyards: None. Fruit wines and wines made from California grapes.

Home winemaking and beermaking supplies, wine glasses, and bar equipment.

Visiting: Monday through Friday 10:00 a.m.-9:00 p.m. all year. Saturday, Sunday 10:00 a.m.-7:00 p.m.

Storage capacity: 8,000 gallons.

Directions: North from Hwy. 30 on Story St. to Eighth. Right turn past Citizens Bank, to 926.

Private Stock Winery was once an opera house named Virginia. Rose Larson tells of the wealthy Boone citizen who gave the town not one, but three opera houses, each named after one of his three daughters. Virginia, the first, went through a number of transformations on the way to becoming a winery. Virginia was even a bakery for awhile.

Tom Larson, formerly a master plumber in Boone and Ames, home of nearby Iowa State University, made wines as a hobby before he became a professional winemaker. Iowa State students are steady customers, and visitors come from coast to coast, Tom says.

Cranberry wine is the general favorite, pineapple is popular, and so are the two rhubarb wines, one dry, one sweet, made of Iowa "pie-plant." Peach wine is made from Georgia peaches, pear wine from Washington State's juiciest fruit. Larson makes wine in twenty-one different flavors, almost as many as an ice cream shop, and he has permits for three hundred. If the buyer wants them, personalized labels can be applied to any of the wines.

Wines of Private Stock Winery

Fruit wines, including blueberry, cherry, bing cherry, cranberry, peach, pineapple, plum, sweet and dry, rhubarb and strawberry, sweet and dry.

WHITE WINE

White Dry and *White Sweet Wine,* California grapes.
Iowa White Sweet, Iowa White Dry Wine, rhubarb.

RED WINE

Cabernet Sauvignon, California grapes, limited bottling.
Concord Sweet Wine
Concord Dry Wine

Price of Wines: $3.85 for most; special cabernet, $12.50.

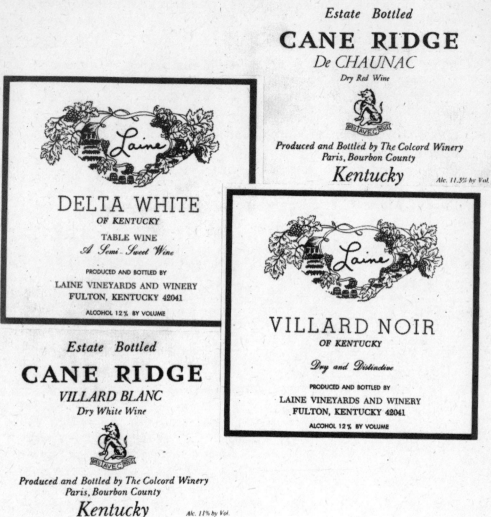

Estate Bottled

CANE RIDGE

De CHAUNAC

Dry Red Wine

Produced and Bottled by The Colcord Winery
Paris, Bourbon County

Kentucky   Alc. 11.5% by Vol.

Laine

DELTA WHITE
OF KENTUCKY

TABLE WINE
A Semi-Sweet Wine

PRODUCED AND BOTTLED BY

LAINE VINEYARDS AND WINERY
FULTON, KENTUCKY 42041

ALCOHOL 12% BY VOLUME

Laine

VILLARD NOIR
OF KENTUCKY

Dry and Distinctive

PRODUCED AND BOTTLED BY

LAINE VINEYARDS AND WINERY
FULTON, KENTUCKY 42041

ALCOHOL 12% BY VOLUME

Estate Bottled

CANE RIDGE

VILLARD BLANC

Dry White Wine

Produced and Bottled by The Colcord Winery
Paris, Bourbon County

Kentucky   Alc. 11% by Vol.

The Wines
of Kentucky

When you think of Kentucky, lots of words and phrases come to mind: old Kentucky home, Kentucky fried chicken, Kentucky blue-grass, horses, Derby, bourbon—but never, well hardly ever—wine. That's going to change.

It's been about 170 years since vines were grown for wine along the Kentucky border of the Ohio River. Now with most restrictive legislation removed, small wineries are beginning to pop up in Kentucky. Bill Oliver, the law professor from Indiana (p. 27), has helped enormously with encouragement and a practical demonstration of what can be done with a strip-mined Kentucky mountain.

In mining for coal in eastern Kentucky, the mountains, in effect, have their tops cut off, shaken out, and turned upside-down. When the coal is gone, a lot of loose rock and shale remains, leaving good cracks and crevices for grape roots to take hold. The Falcon Coal Company celebrated its first harvest in 1975 on the first strip-mined mountain planted to Oliver's mist-propagated French hybrid vines. The wine had been made at the Oliver Winery in Indiana, as it has been each year since then. The first harvest was officially celebrated after the bottling, by the Governor of Kentucky and leading citizens of the state, including members of environmental protection societies who had opposed strip-mining in the Kentucky hills.

Restoring beauty to nature while creating a new industry in a poverty-stricken area is an exciting development. Also, the wines are good, and getting better every year.

Oliver says it will take twenty years to tell how this experiment is going. He hopes to interest the University of Kentucky, and possibly a commercial group who might want to establish a mountain winery, for it is difficult to work long distance. Oliver believes that the wines should be made in Kentucky, his home state, rather than in Indiana.

With his guidance and example, the state of Kentucky enacted legislation to permit the establishment of small wineries. The first two are doing very well.

Colcord Winery, Inc.
ESTABLISHED 1976

P.O. Box K, Third and Pleasant Streets, Paris, KY 40361

Phone: 606-987-7440

Owner, F. Carlton Colcord. President and winemaker, Helen Turley.

Vineyards: 37 acres French hybrids; some vinifera.

Visiting: Afternoons Tuesday-Sunday. Closed for winter, except by appointment.

Storage capacity: 7,000 gallons.

Directions: Downtown Paris, 18 miles northeast of Lexington.

Colcord Winery was opened November 11, 1977, with the introduction of four young wines under the Cane Ridge label. Owner F. Carlton Colcord was reared in Bourbon County, and Cane Ridge is his family's favorite farm. Colcord's career has been in the international oil business since he took his degree in chemistry from the University of Kentucky, but his interest in wine grapes dates from residence in Italy. He now divides his time between London, where the Colcord children are in school and where business interests remain, and his Kentucky vineyards and winery.

Mature vinifera wines are producing at Colcord and one day there will be enough grapes for commercial wine. Colcord wines are made naturally and aged in Kentucky oak.

Wines of Colcord

WHITE WINE

Kentucky White, mostly aurora, dry.
Villard Blanc, dry.

RED WINE

Chelois, dry (will age).
De Chaunac, dry (will age).
Kentucky Red, chelois and De Chaunac, dry.

Price of wines: $5.00-$5.50.

Laine Vineyards and Winery
ESTABLISHED 1978

RFD Box 247, Fulton, KY 42041

Phone: 502-472-3345

Owner, president, Paul A. Laine, Jr.; vice-president, Jane Laine.

Vineyards: 54 acres.

Visiting: 8:00 a.m.-5:00 p.m. daily all year. Closed Sunday.

Storage capacity: 50,000 gallons.

Directions: 2 miles west of Fulton, KY on SR 166.

After a thirty-year career in electronics, Paul Laine was able to retire from one executive position to another which had been a sideline for several years. His plantings of French-American hybrid grape varieties date back to 1973, so Laine Vineyards and Winery soon became a reality. As anyone might guess, Jane Laine is well involved in the business and social aspects of the winery, too.

The Laines have three married daughters who, though not involved, enjoy sampling the product.

Most plantings and wines are hybrid varieties, though vinifera planted so far are doing well. There's an acre of grey riesling, and other viniferas unusual for the location include chenin blanc, french colombard, and barbera. Native grapes? Several acres of delaware for wines and half-an-acre of concord for Jane's jellies and jams.

Most red wines are aged in fifty-gallon white oak barrels; there are also two 1500-gallon white oak tanks for aging. White wines wait about a month in stainless steel. The Laines have a very modern, well-equipped winery. As their first 10,000 gallons of commercial wine were bottled in the fall of 1979, it is obvious that the best is yet to come from this Kentucky winery.

Wines of Laine Winery

WHITE WINE

Aurora
Vidal Blanc
Villard Blanc

RED WINE

Baco Noir
De Chaunac
Villard Noir

Price of Wines: $3.00-$4.00.

The Wines
of Michigan

Michigan is a huge fruit bowl. Apples, blueberries, cherries, peaches, and apricots are important commercial crops. Grapes are also part of this list. Michigan's concord production has always been enormous; once most of her wines were made of this native grape. Only in recent years have Michigan wine buffs noticed that the concord tide is running more to juice and jam and less to wine, though wine production is increasing steadily.

Recently, several progressive Michigan winemakers were angered when a Detroit-area columnist wrote that Michigan wines were not fit to drink, "because they are all made of concord grapes." The column was headlined "Michigan Wines—Ugh!" These men challenged both writer and publisher, set up some wine-tastings and opened more than a few eyes and palates to the much-improved quality of the state's wines and to unfamiliar labels such as vidal, de Chaunac, white riesling.

Concord wines still have their partisans, and as long as there is a demand, a few wineries will continue to make them. Concord wines nowadays are usually improved with California wine in the blend.

Michigan winemakers set their own individual goals of quality. For a few, that means growing only classical grapes. For most it means making a knowledgeable selection among the hybrid grapes well adapted to their vineyard sites.

Michigan's two peninsulas border four of the five Great Lakes, and the state is liberally sprinkled top to bottom with smaller lakes. So, is it any wonder that Michigan is a mecca for water sports enthusiasts, skiers, fishermen, and sightseers? Most wineries are situated near the roads to popular resort areas, and winery-visiting is becoming an important recreation in itself.

Good Harbor Vineyards, Lake Leelanau, was scheduled to join the cluster of Leelanau County wineries in the spring of 1980. Owner Bruce Simpson, son of a Michigan fruit grower, has a degree from Michigan State in horticulture and agribusiness, has studied enology at University of California, Davis. Good Harbor is across the lake (Leelanau) from Bernard Rink's pioneering Boskydel Vineyard. There's a farm market adjoining the winery and tasting room. Fresh fruits and vegetables, homemade jams, and bakery goods are available.

Black River Winery at Southfield may not open until 1984 or 1985, for owners Michael J. and Nancy Firosz are taking a slow, computer-guided approach to their project, which was started in 1970. Firosz is a management consultant of Troy, Michigan, who began his efforts by studying the soils and microclimates of Michigan until he located what he deemed to be the perfect 10 acres. That took four years. Now many varieties of grapes, both hybrids and special clones of white riesling and chardonnay are well established, and Firosz has leased 40 acres more and established a nursery. This enterprise will be an interesting one to watch.

Spartan Cellars is not a commercial winery, but comprises the testing grounds of the state's viticultural research program at Michigan State University, Lansing. It is guided by Dr. Gordon (Stan) Howell, a genial man well known to all of Michigan's winegrowers and winemakers. Dozens of grape varieties are under study at the university and at Sodus, a research station in the heart of Michigan's famous fruit belt.

Grape research at Michigan State is directed toward finding cold-hardy, disease resistant varieties that, above all, make good wine.

Boskydel Vineyard
ESTABLISHED 1976

Rt. 1, Box 522, Lake Leelanau, MI 49653

Phone: 616-256-9544

Owner-Winemaker, Bernard C. Rink.

Vineyard: 20 acres hybrids.

Visiting: 1:00 p.m.-6:00 p.m. daily.

Storage capacity: 20,000 gallons.

Directions: M-22 north from Traverse City to Suttons Bay; left on M-204. Just before Shell station, left into Co. Rd. 641. Drive about 3 miles. On left, overlooking Lake Leelanau.

Bernard Rink's winery and vineyards benefit not only from the marine climate of big Lake Michigan, only three miles away, but also from the warmer waters of the smaller Lake Leelanau, which is about twenty miles long. Boskydel, set among pine trees on a hill, overlooks Lake Leelanau; it can boast one of the most beautiful sites for a winery in the country.

This is cherryland, U.S.A., but Rink's wines are not cherry wines. For fourteen years he has been growing French-American hybrids, and he has had enough time to discover which of thirty varieties planted experimentally do best on his twenty acres of land. They are vignoles (Ravat 51), seyval blanc, and Seibel 10868 (a grape still carrying the hybridizer's name and the numbers of the cross) for white wines. For red wines, Rink has selected De Chaunac, chancellor, and cascade.

Rink says that baco noir, a successful grape for other Michigan growers, is susceptible to crown-gall in his territory, while chelois, also much used by other Michigan wineries, doesn't produce the quality he seeks. Angelo Spinazze makes a beautiful Maréchal Foch at Bronte Winery, but Foch made on Lake Leelanau has a grassy taste, Bernie Rink comments. That might be due to the cellar treatment, he admits, but he has discontinued the wine.

Recently a French oil company executive bought nineteen cases of Boskydel Vignoles and rosé wines, telling Bernie Rink that they were the closest he could come to the wines he drinks in France.

A different microclimate exists just a half-mile away from his favored spot, and a retired chemistry professor, who grows grapes on Lake Michigan's shores four miles away from Boskydel, finds that the fruit ripens two weeks later in a climate ten degrees cooler.

Rink thinks he may try for riesling on one-and-one-half acres at the brow of his hill where the sensitive vines will be protected by pine trees but still be exposed to sun.

Bernie and Suzanne Rink have grown their own vineyard workers—five sons, three of them teen-agers, all of whom help in the various aspects of wine-growing and wine-making. Relatives and friends lend a hand happily at harvest time.

The unusual name of the winery reflects family sentiment. Boskydel was named for "The Elves of Bosky Dingle," stories that the Rink children have always loved. Rink is library director for Northwest Michigan College, Traverse City, Michigan.

Wines of Boskydel Vineyard

WHITE WINE

Seyval Blanc, dry, fruity.
Vignoles, fruity when young; mellow with age.

RED WINE

Boskydel Rosé, a blend of five hybrids.
De Chaunac Rosé, slightly sweet.
De Chaunac, dry, fruity when young; develops bouquet with age.

Price of wines: $3.35-$4.65.

Bronte Champagne and Wines Co., Inc.
ESTABLISHED 1933

Hartford, MI 49057 (Business office is in Detroit)

Phone: 616-621-3419

President and general manager, Robert E. Wozniak; vice-president and winemaker, Angelo Spinazze; chemist, Curtis Frick.

Vineyards: 230 acres hybrids, delaware, catawba.

Visiting: Tours and tasting, all year, 10:00 a.m.-4:00 p.m. daily; noon to 4:00 p.m. Sundays.

Storage capacity: 1,000,000 gallons.

Directions: I-94 between Chicago and Detroit, off at exit 46, Hartford, 5 miles south to Keeler.

Bronte is one of the most interesting wineries in the Midwest for a number of reasons, the first being the winery's historical background. The vineyards were planted in 1944 and 1945, by German prisoners of war. Prior to that, the winery bought all of its grapes from growers. The vineyard site was a racetrack between 1901 and 1913. Socially prominent Midwesterners patronized the famous "Keeler Donnybrook" harness races. One of the winery buildings, in earlier days, was the headquarters of the Michigan Chapter of the Women's Christian Temperance Union.

The winery was founded by Dr. Theodore Wozniak, a dentist, father of Bronte President Robert Wozniak, exactly twenty-five days after the repeal of Prohibition, May 26, 1933. The name Bronte was retained from a Prohibition-era Detroit company, owned by Wozniak, which produced a non-alcoholic extract. Bronte's business offices remain in Detroit.

Robert Wozniak is credited with starting the "cold duck" wine-drinking boom of a few years ago. He was first to bottle the popular wine cocktail, which had been sold in Detroit restaurants for many years. Other wineries followed and before we could scream for help, the entire country was awash in a combination of sparkling red-and-white wine, sweet and labrusca-flavored. Bronte's original cold duck is still made along with the other *charmat* process sparkling wines, for which the company is well known, and Bronte's may still be better cold duck than any of its imitators.* None of them resembles the German *"kalte ente,"* a combination of still and sparkling white wines usually served in a pitcher with a trailing curl of lemon peel. The Pontchartrain Wine Cellar in Detroit still makes cold duck cocktails with one-third red still wine and two-thirds sparkling white.

Angelo Spinazze, born in Italy to a wine-making family and trained there in enology, came to Bronte by way of the Windsor Wine Company in Canada. He has guided the Bronte winegrowing and winemaking since 1937. Never a man to be content with past performance, he has been a leader in switching from native to hybrid grapes for better

* Grapes used do not include concord; they are *delaware, elvira,* and *white* hybrid grapes.

wines. Bronte was first in the Midwest with a red wine made from Baco No. 1. Spinazze planted baco vines in 1954. A 100 percent varietal, the wine didn't sell as "Baco Dinner Wine," but when the French "noir" was placed on the label, it "took off," Spinazze says. He is ably assisted by Curtis Frick, chemist.

   Bronte vineyards lie around a cluster of small lakes called "Sister Lakes," and the company hopes to build a "Sister Lakes image" for quality.

Wines of Bronte

Generically labeled Wines: chablis, burgundy, Rhine wine, etc.
Sherries, including *Cocktail Sherry, Hartford Cream Sherry.*
Ports, including *White Port, Kosher Port, Hartford Light Port.*
Sparkling Wines, including *Brut Champagne, Cold Duck.*

WHITE WINE

Aurora Blanc
Beau Blanc, (aurora and vidal).
Vidal Blanc

RED WINE

Baco Noir
Beau Rouge, (*Foch, De Chaunac*).
Maréchal Foch
Scarlet Rosé (blend of hybrids).
Pink Catawba
Pink Delaware

Price of Wines: $2.00-$4.00.

Chateau Grand Travers, Ltd.
ESTABLISHED 1976

12239 Center Road, Traverse City, MI 49684

Phone: 616-223-7355

Owner, O'Keefe Centre, Ltd; president, Edward O'Keefe; enologist, Roland Pflager.

Vineyards: 55 acres planted to white vinifera; more being planted.

Visiting: Daily 10:00 a.m.-5:00 p.m., Sunday noon-5:00 p.m.

Storage capacity: 40,000 gallons.

Directions: 7½ miles north of crossing of U.S. 31 and M-37, on M-37.

Chateau Grand Travers sits on a hill, on Old Mission Peninsula, the long pencil of land that juts out from Traverse City into the middle of Grand Traverse Bay. It shares with Boskydel, Leelanau Wine Cellars, and Mawby Vineyards the watery benefits of northwest Michigan. However, it is even more protected, Ed O'Keefe says, as winter temperatures of Grand Travers are from five to seven degrees warmer. In the viciously cold winter of '79, the thermometer hit thirty-eight below zero in Traverse City one night. It sank to nine below in his vineyards for just half an hour, O'Keefe says. Then, it rose to fifteen above. There was bud damage to twenty-five per cent of his crop, but he remains determined to grow only vinifera.

While establishing his winery and vineyards, O'Keefe was a distributor of European and California wines in the Detroit area, warehousing them in the winery. His first wines were from apples, cherries and shipped grapes, not unusual before a winery's own vines come into bearing. For awhile, there seemed to be a swinging door for vineyard managers and enologists but the rather flamboyant O'Keefe believes that he now knows the way to go. Vinifera only—chardonnay, and especially white riesling from which some beautiful fresh and late-picked wines already have been made. Now other varieties are going into the Peninsula soil—Germany's scheurebe, müller-thurgau, and the Alsatian gewürztraminer, which is thriving in a few other Midwestern vineyards. Also, he wants to try muscat ottonel, a variety that Konstantin Frank introduced to Eastern winegrowers some time ago. It does well in cold climates, and makes sweet, flowery wines which many enjoy.

O'Keefe has banished his "chablis," "burgundy," and "rhine wine" labels and will make no more California zinfandel or cabernet sauvignon, though he says he's thinking of finding a little place in California to crush chenin blanc, to add to his stable. At present, he has only the chardonnay and riesling, but makes them in various styles. A late-picked chardonnay, called "Sweet Nancy" after his wife, is a rich *beerenauslese* type, but note that it is made with chardonnay, not riesling. That is unusual. He has made "eiswein" (from grapes quick-frozen on the vine) and other specialties from late harvest riesling. Quantities of the special wines are limited.

Wines of Chateau Grand Travers

Chardonnay
White Riesling

Price of wines: $7.00-$10.00.

Fenn Valley Vineyards
ESTABLISHED 1973

122nd Ave., Fennville, MI 49408

Phone: 616-561-2396

Owner and president, William Welsch; vice president-business manager, Wesley Sievert; winemaker-farm manager, Douglas Welsch.

Vineyards, orchards: 70 acres hybrids, vinifera.

Home winemaking supplies.

Visiting: Daily 10:00 a.m.-5:00 p.m. Sunday 1:00 a.m.-5:00 p.m., May through November. Special programs for groups by arrangement.

Storage capacity: 100,000 gallons.

Directions: I-196 to Fennville Exit 34, east 3½ miles to 62nd St., south 1 mile to 122nd Ave.

The Welsch family had an environmental problem, in 1973, when they bought the 230-acre fruit farm near Fennville, which they transformed "almost overnight" into Fenn Valley Vineyards and Wine Cellar. It is now one of the most attractive wineries to visit anywhere, but it took a lot of hard work.

Not far inland from the eastern shore of Lake Michigan, set on hillsides with sandy soil, the location is ideal as a site for a winery planning estate-bottled production of wines from hybrid and vinifera grapes. It is also only a few miles from Holland, the famous Michigan tulip town, whose festival draws thousands of visitors each spring, and it is not far off the tourist routes which take more thousands to northern Michigan's resort country for winter skiing and summer water sports. However, despite its perfect location, the farm had been abandoned and allowed to deteriorate. Young Douglas Welsch, farm manager and winemaker for the family, had to clear twenty-seven acres of broken, diseased peach and cherry trees before the soil could be prepared for Fenn Valley's first plantings. Not only that, but the farm had been used as a junkyard.

"I'd go to the dump every week with a load of old bed springs, refrigerators, stoves, and parts of junked cars," says Douglas, a former biology teacher.

Fenn Valley is a subsidiary of Welsch Lumber and Supply Company of Mokena, Illinois, of which William Welsch, Doug's father, is president. Bill Welsch is also the key figure in managing the winery and marketing its product. Fenn Valley is a distinct family operation. The senior Welsches, Douglas and his wife Lynn, who teaches school in Fennville, have built homes close to the winery which is everything a winery should be. Built into a hillside, it is spacious and attractive, with a tasting room and self-guided tour facilities.

Ruth Welsch, Bill's wife and Douglas' mother, describes herself as "having graduated from school marm to barmaid." She is the gracious, attractive hostess in the wine-tasting room. Two daughters, Deborah and Diana, college students, help at the winery as much as they can.

Fenn Valley has over fifty acres in hybrids and vinifera with plans for planting another seventy acres. Twenty acres of fruit orchard in good condition were spared from the bulldozer, and from these trees the Welsches at first made cherry and peach wines. They also made blueberry, strawberry, plum, and pear wines from local fruits—true fruit wines, they will tell you. Then, as grape crops matured, all fruit wines but peach and blueberry were phased out.

Wines of Fenn Valley

Estate-bottled vinifera and hybrid grape wines as plantings mature. Fenn Valley natural, true fruit wines: blueberry, peach.

WHITE WINE

Vin Blanc, principally seyval blanc; soft, fruity, dry.
Regal White, a blend of seyval and vidal blanc grapes. Semi-dry.
White Riesling, made in classic German style.
Gewürztraminer, spicy, full-bodied with residual sweetness.
Vidal Blanc, soft, dry, German-style.

RED WINE

Vin Rosé, lightly dry, fruity.
Regal Red, chancellor-Foch blend.
Fenn Valley Red, a dry blend of hybrid grapes.
Ruby Red, soft, fruity, chillable.
Chancellor, dry, full-bodied Bordeaux-style.
Mulled wine, with spices and fruit juices added.

Price of wines: Most $3.25-$5.25. Gewürztraminer, $6.75, White Riesling, $7.50. You may have personalized labels printed while you wait, at the winery, 5 labels for $1.00.

Fink Winery
ESTABLISHED 1976

208 Main St., Dundee, MI 48138

Phone: 313-529-3296

Owner, Carl E. Fink.

Vineyards: None. Wines are made from concentrates and Michigan honey.

Home winemaking supplies.

Visiting: 9:00 a.m.-5:00 p.m. daily except Sunday.

Storage capacity: 4,000 gallons.

Directions: U.S. 23 midway between Ann Arbor and Toledo, Ohio. Off at Dundee exit; to center of town; right on Main St. 1 block.

Most of Michigan's wineries lie near the eastern shore of Lake Michigan, whose winds and waters are protective of grapevines. The Fink Winery is located near the western end of Lake Erie, but neither prevailing winds nor warming waters matter very much, because Fink's wines are not made from homegrown grapes, but from grape concentrates and honey.

Carl, a teacher of data processing in a Toledo high school, and his brother Gary, an engineer, were accustomed to helping their dad, Howard Fink, in the winemaker's supply shop he had operated in the town of Dundee for twelve years. So when the senior Fink retired in 1972, the sons took over the shop.

Howard Fink is not involved in the winemaking, "but he gives plenty of advice from home," laughs Carl, a good-natured bachelor. "We're Michigan's smallest winery," he says.

Being small and without vineyards has its advantages. There are no worries about weather, birds, or rabbits, which gives more time to be friendly with the customers. Dundee, with a population of less than 2,500 citizens, lies an equidistant twenty-five miles between Ann Arbor and Toledo, both famous centers of higher education. One might assume that the Fink Winery would be patronized largely by the college crowd, but that isn't true, the Fink brothers say. Their patrons are of all ages and descriptions.

Mead, which Mary and Bill Oliver in Indiana find exceptionally popular with university students, also is a favorite at the Michigan winery. Carl Fink makes his mead with "raw, unfiltered, uncooked Michigan honey," and sweetens a grenache rosé and a White Nectar (blended California white grapes) with honey. He ages California zinfandel in wood for a honey-sweetened red wine.

Wines of Fink Winery

Fruit Wines: Apple and sour cherry.

WHITE WINE

Chablis
Chateau Blanc

Mead, made of Michigan honey.
White Nectar, California grape wine with natural honey flavoring added.

RED WINE

Concord
Ruby Red
Rosé 'n Honey, California grenache grape wine with natural honey flavoring added.
Zinfandel 'n Honey, a semi-dry California zinfandel wine with natural honey flavoring added.

Price of wines: Under $2.00.

Frontenac Vineyards, Inc.
ESTABLISHED 1933

3418 W. Michigan Ave., Paw Paw, MI 49079

Phone: 616-657-5531

President, Edward J. Wieferman; plant manager, Carl Corsi.

Vineyards: None. Wines made from purchased grapes and juices.

Visiting: Daily 9:00 a.m.-5:00 p.m.; Sunday noon-5:00 p.m. Last hourly tour at 4:00 p.m.

Storage capacity: 650,000 gallons.

Directions: Exit 56 on I-94, 1 mile north to Red Arrow Highway, right turn, just outside city limits of Paw Paw on Red Arrow Highway.

Frontenac was a family-owned winery, until 1967. It has changed hands twice since then, and capacity has now been expanded. Despite its name, Frontenac has no vineyards of its own, but purchases from growers grapes and fruits for fruit wines.

Frontenac has a tasting room in connection with its retail store. There are more than forty wines in the firm's two lines. Recently Frontenac has been importing Italian wine for its "Always Elvis" label portraying the late entertainer, Elvis Presley. The three Elvis wines are popular with fans of the "king of rock and roll."

Wines of Frontenac

Generically labeled wines, burgundy, chablis, niagara rhine wine; apple, apricot, berry, plum, and other fruit wines; port, sherry, sangria, "Liebfraugarten."
"Smash" Line, Cherry Smash, Strawberry Smash, and others.

Price of wines: Most around $2.00.

Lakeside Vineyard, Inc.
ESTABLISHED 1975

13581 Red Arrow Highway, Harbert, MI 49115

Phone: 616-469-0700

President, Cecil E. Pond; Winemaker, Art Sandtviet.

Vineyard: 4 acres; most grapes purchased from growers.

Wine garden.

Visiting: Daily 9:00 a.m.-5:00 p.m.; Sunday noon-5:00 p.m. Private tours for groups of 10 or more by reservation. Phone Maxine Wood, or write for information.

Storage capacity: 500,000 gallons.

Directions: I-94, exit 12, ½ mile to Red Arrow Highway, 1 mile left to Harbert and winery.

A few years ago, when Lakeside Vineyard was the Molly Pitcher Winery, its wines were mostly sweet concord wines and concord-based specialties of higher alcohol content, such as "Peppermint Twist" and "Cherry Jubilee." The owners were health food enthusiasts who didn't drink wine themselves.*

---

* The proprietor retired as he approached his ninetieth birthday so that the couple could travel. It was too late to turn the winery over to their son, who was sixty-five and also wished to retire.

The Pond Family makes much better wine from concord and niagara grapes. They have kept a Molly Pitcher line, lightened in taste by blending California wine with the native grape juices, and no longer cooked to death for "sanitation."

The women who pour wines in Lakeside's attractive "Wine Barrel" tasting room and outdoor wine garden dress in bonnets and full skirts as the legendary Molly Pitcher, Revolutionary heroine, might have been dressed while carrying water to the colonial forces on that steamy-hot day in 1778 when the battle of Monmouth was fought. They are charming hostesses.

The owners are looking for more vineyard land to supplement their four acres. At present, most grapes are purchased from growers and Lakeside is buying some hybrid grapes as well as the native varieties.

Public relations director Maxine Wood stirs up all kinds of activities for spring, summer, and fall weekends at the winery. They include a Maifest, a fine arts fair in August, and an Oktoberfest. These events draw thousands to the tasting room and the charming wine garden. There are picnics and musical events as well as tours and tastings. Little Lakeside is a fun place to visit, and only seventy-five miles from Chicago.

Wines of Lakeside Vineyard

(Two labels: Lakeside, Molly Pitcher. Sherries and Ports.)

WHITE WINE

Niagara
Val Blanc

RED WINE

Concord
Val Rosé
Val Rouge
Romantique Cream Sherry

Many other wines, about 30 in all, also available.

Price of wines: $2.15-$6.99.

Leelanau Wine Cellars Ltd.
ESTABLISHED 1975

726 Memorial Highway, Traverse City, MI 49684

Phone: 616-946-1653

Owners, Charles Kalchik, Michael Jacobson; winemaker, Nathan Stackhouse.

Vineyards: 20 acres hybrids, 45 acres vinifera, 2,000 acres fruit trees.

Visiting: 10:00 a.m.-6:00 p.m. daily; Sunday, noon-6:00 p.m.

Storage capacity: 70,000 gallons.

Directions: 1 mile north of Junction of highways 31 and 37, 5 miles south of Traverse City.

Leelanau County is a delight to the eye. In spring, when fruit trees burst into flamboyant color, Leelanau Wine Cellars contributes to that beauty with its 2,000 acres of fruit farms. However, fruit wines aren't the only kind made at this new winery. Owners Charles Kalchik and Michael Jacobson have also planted forty-five acres of vinifera grapes and twenty acres of hybrids.

The wines are being made by Nathan Stackhouse, Leelanau's enologist, former winemaker for both Warner and St. Julian. Stackhouse has Cabernet Sauvignon and Leon Millot wines developing for Leelanau, which expects to "go heavy on the reds." He is particularly proud of his Baco Noir 1978.

The actual Leelanau Wine Cellars are at Omena, on the Leelanau Peninsula looking eastward over Grand Traverse Bay. Crushing, fermenting, and bottling take place there. The visitors' center, tasting and sales facilities are more easily found. They top a hill in a very convenient spot, just north of the junction of highways 31 and 37, running into and out of the attractive Michigan resort and cherry center, Traverse City.

The Wines of Leelanau Wine Cellars

Fruit Wines: Apple, cherry, pear, plum, strawberry and nectarine.

WHITE WINE

Aurora
Chardonnay
Leelanau White
Seyval Blanc
Vignoles

RED WINE

Baco Noir
Cabernet Sauvignon
Chelois
De Chaunac
Leelanau Red
Leelanau Rosé
Merlot

Price of wines: $2.70-$4.50.

L. Mawby Vineyards-Winery
ESTABLISHED 1977

4519 Elm Valley Road, Suttons Bay, MI 49682

Phone: 616-271-3522

Owner, Lawrence Mawby.

Vineyards: 14 acres French hybrids; 1½ acres vinifera.

Visiting: By appointment. (Directions given to those making appointments).

Storage capacity: 3,500 gallons.

Larry Mawby fell naturally into winegrowing, because he and his parents own a 600-acre farm. He personally owned "a couple of hundred" acres of apple, cherry, and peach orchards, and wanted to diversify. "I was interested in wine as a consumer," he says, "so the obvious answer was grapes."

   Mawby designed and built his own winery and lives above it. "I'm small and I'm going to stay small," he says. For white wines, he planted aurora, seyval blanc, and vignoles, all of which are developing well. His red wines, in addition to Foch, will be chancellor, chelois, and de Chaunac. The Foch vineyard produces a rich wine that Larry likes, though he's aware that Bernie Rink, only three miles away on the Leelanau Peninsula, has rejected Foch. "The soils are very different," says Mawby. He went to Oregon in order to find the vinifera clones he wanted to plant. He believes that Oregon viticulturists are well advanced in clone selection, and though winters are warmer in Oregon and the growing season is longer, growing conditions in many ways parallel those on the Leelanau Peninsula. Mawby is cultivating eight different pinot noir clones, two chardonnay clones, as well as nursery stock from Swiss and French vineyards.

A cheerful and positive young man, he doesn't plan to make fruit wines other than apple, though he'd make a sparkling apple wine if it weren't for the federal tax "on bubbles," which is five times that for still wine. Mawby will make 100% varietal wines or blends, depending upon what works best each harvest season.

Wines of L. Mawby Vineyards

WHITE WINE

Seyval Blanc, 1980.
Vignoles, 1980.
L. Mawby White (vignoles, Seyval Blanc).

RED WINE

L. Mawby Red (Foch-de Chaunac blanc).
Foch, 1979.
Picnic Rosé (Foch blend).

Price of wines: Under $4.50.

St. Julian & La Salle Winery
ESTABLISHED 1921

716 Kalamazoo St., Paw Paw, MI 49079

Phone: 616-657-5568

Board chairman, Paul Braganini; president and general manager, David Braganini; winemaker, Charles Catherman.

Vineyards: None. Grapes are bought from growers.

Storage capacity: 1,500,000 gallons.

Visiting: Daily 9:00 a.m.-5:00 p.m.; Sunday 12:00 p.m.-5:00 p.m.

Deli and Cheese Shop.

Tours daily 9:30 a.m.-4:30 p.m., every half hour. Tours take half an hour.

Directions: Paw Paw exit from I-94, in downtown Paw Paw. Warner and St. Julian are next-door neighbors.

St. Julian, Michigan's oldest winery, was reborn from the ashes of fire and tragedy in the seventies. St. Julian's offices, hospitality room, and general storage facilities burned to the ground in May of 1972.

I interviewed seventy-seven-year-old Mariano Meconi, founder of the firm once known as the Italian Wine Company,* and his son Eugene, president of St. Julian, a month or two later. We sat on cases of wine in a trailer, which served as the temporary headquarters during rebuilding. Eugene Meconi was just out of the hospital after open-heart surgery, and he was composing a letter to growers, telling them that St. Julian would crush in the fall even if it had to use the presses of competitors.

Then, double tragedy followed the disaster of the fire. Eugene Meconi died, and so did his brother Robert, who was vice-president. Their sister Julia had preceded them in death. There was no second generation of Meconis to succeed Mariano, who was ready to retire.

Though he had established another business in Pennsylvania, Paul Braganini, Julia's widower, was called upon to take over. A happier event ensued when Paul Braganini and Phyllis Meconi, Eugene's widow, married and combined their two families, which totaled eight children. Now, there's an active third generation participating in the increasingly better fortunes of this solid old wine company. The new facilities are attractive and efficient. The winery is dedicated to Eugene Meconi, Robert Meconi, and Julia Meconi Braganini.

* The puzzling Prohibition date of founding is explained by the fact that Meconi started his winery in Windsor, Ontario. He later moved it to Detroit where he made sacramental wines during the dry years, and eventually moved to Paw Paw.

St. Julian, under the guidance of Mariano Meconi's grandson, David Braganini, makes wines from many kinds of grapes, hybrids and traditional native varieties. And since 1975 St. Julian has been transformed from a winery making mostly dessert wines to a major producer of Michigan premium table wines.

Wines of St. Julian and La Salle

Fruit and Berry Wines
Sparkling Wines, bulk or charmat method, most from native grapes, one from vidal blanc.
Flor Sherry and other sherries and ports.
Sholom Kosher Wine

WHITE WINE

Rhine Wine, Sauterne, others from native grapes.
Vidal Blanc
Seyval Blanc
Friars' Blanc

RED WINE

Friars' Noir, Friars' Rosé, blends of French hybrids.
Mellow Red, Robust Burgundy, other wines from native grapes.
Chancellor Noir
Maréchal Foch

Price of wines: Most under $2.00. Vidal Blanc champagne, $4.75; Flor Sherry, $6.50.

Tabor Hill Vineyard and Winecellar Inc.

ESTABLISHED 1970

Rt. 1, Box 746, Buchanan, MI 49107

Phone: 616-422-1161

Owner, Chi Company; chief executive, chairman, David F. Upton;

president and winemaster, Leonard R. Olson (former owner); vineyard manager, Tim Cote.

Vineyard: 45 acres in hybrids and vinifera; grapes also purchased from growers under contract.

Visiting: Daily, 11:00 a.m.-6:00 p.m. Tours every half hour, noon to 5:00 p.m.

Restaurant, picnic facilities. (Phone for restaurant information. Lunches and special dinners on weekends.)

Storage capacity: 60,000 gallons.

Directions: I-94, Bridgman exit. Follow signs.

Leonard Olson's success with white (Johannisberg) riesling is such that he has made a country-wide impression. While waiting for his own riesling vines to mature, he bought grapes from John Moorhead of North East, Pennsylvania. With the 1977 vintage this ex-steel salesman had an estate-bottled, vintage-dated Johannisberg riesling in typical German style, though limited in production.

Tabor Hill plantings were begun in 1968, and Len and Ellen Olson, their four children, and numerous relatives and friends celebrated their first vintage in 1972. The wines made from that vintage were seyval blanc, vidal blanc, and baco noir. A year later, Olson made both chardonnay and riesling. His chardonnay is almost as remarkable as the riesling, and of course in limited supply. There is even a little cabernet sauvignon to brag about, most unusual for Michigan.

The basic wines of Tabor Hill are Cuvée Blanc, predominantly riesling, Cuuvée Rouge and Cuvée Rosé hybrid blends. The rosé is made with a touch of California petite sirah in the blend. Wines from hybrid grapes are aged in oak and given as much care as the vinifera varieties.

The hilltop winery is a contemporary "chateau" built of rough-hewn cedar planks. Within, the spacious tasting room blends old with new by means of the heavy beams and time-silvered siding from the 100-year-old barn the winery replaced. Below are the functional parts of the winery, the crushing, fermenting, and bottling equipment, the casks that hold the aging wines.

By happy chance, a master craftsman in wood lives just a few miles from Tabor Hill. T.C. Cavey has carved an oak cask for each year the winery has been in business; the 1970 cask depicts early plantings. Later carvings show wine-tasting, Bacchus smiling over a good harvest, and other related themes. This kind of thing is fairly common in Germany and in the sherry district of Spain. In Michigan it is unique.

Tom Olson, Chicago artist and designer, is Len's younger brother. He opens his exhibitions at the winery, then moves them to Chicago galleries. Tom's wedding took place at Tabor Hill, a beautiful site for any wedding. One young couple married there left wedding guests right after the ceremony to bowl with their league, then returned to Tabor Hill for the celebration of their marriage.

Tabor Hill is the setting for many barbecues and picnics and several wining and dining societies have held all-day wine fests there. The hospitality at Tabor Hill Vineyard is warm and wonderful.

In 1979, ownership changed, but Olson is still in charge and making the wines of Tabor Hill.

Wines of Tabor Hill Vineyard

WHITE WINE

Cuvée Blanc
Chardonnay, limited estate bottling.
Chardonnay ("American," from Washington state grapes).
Gewürztraminer (Washington grapes).
Riesling and Late-picked Riesling, estate bottled.
Vidal-Riesling (riesling is from Washington grapes).
Vidal Blanc: sec, demi-sec, and Late Harvest (3 wines).
Ice Wine, limited estate bottling.

RED WINE

Baco Noir: Winemaster's Selection, Nouveau, Reserve (3 wines).
Cuvée Rouge and Cuvée Rosé
Cabernet Sauvignon (Washington Grapes).

Price of Wines: Cuvée wines, $2.85. Others up to $6.00. Vinifera varietals, $10-$14. Ice wine $25.00.

Vendramino Vineyards Company
<small>ESTABLISHED 1976</small>

Rt. 4, Paw Paw, MI 49079

Phone: 616-657-5890

Owner, John J. Coleman.

Vineyard: None. French hybrids and native grapes purchased.

Visiting: Open April 1-November 1. Monday-Saturday, 11:00 a.m.-5:00 p.m.; Sunday noon-5:00 p.m. Self-guided tours.

Amateur winemaking equipment; also grape juice for home wine-making.

Storage capacity: 5,000 gallons.

Directions: I-94 to Paw Paw exit 56, north ¼ mile.

John Coleman, mechanical engineer for Ford Motor Company in Dearborn, wants his winery to be more than a winery—he wants it to be a place for people to congregate and have fun. When we talked with him just before his opening on July 2, 1977, he was up to his ears in carpenters who were building a 1200-square-foot tasting room addition to his new winery. It houses a tasting bar forty-five feet long.

Plans were also afoot for a grape stomp contest between two universities, Northern Michigan at Marquette, and Western in Kalamazoo. Teams of six students would stomp in a 1500-gallon tank, the champion winning a $100 bond for the school and a trophy, the "purple foot award."

Since then there have been several more grape festivals, and Vendramino wines have won a number of medals at the Michigan State Fair.

People who visit the winery may buy lunch of bread, Wisconsin cheese, Detroit sausage and wine, then sit at picnic tables to enjoy it.

Football fan Coleman has permits to label wines in honor of eighteen top teams. "M-Go-Blue" is for University of Michigan, for example, and "Spartan Magic" for Michigan State. Except for the Concord, all wines are made of French hybrids.

Wines of Vendramino Vineyards

Apple cider, Onion wine (for seasoning)

WHITE WINE

M-Go-Blue, semi-sweet.
Vendramino White
Seyval Blanc, dry.

RED WINE

Ol' Paw Paw, sweet concord.
Spartan Magic, rosé.
Vendramino Red and *Rosé*

Price of wines: $2.69.

Warner Vineyards Inc.
ESTABLISHED 1939

706 S. Kalamazoo St., Paw Paw, MI 47079

Phone: 616-657-3165

Chairman of board, James K. Warner; president, James J. Warner; secretary-treasurer, Arleta Warner.

Vineyards: 225 acres (including 36 acres in hybrids and vinifera).

Visiting: Tours daily, 9:00 a.m.-5:00 p.m. Tours start on the hour (last tour at 4:00 p.m.); Sunday, noon to 5:00 p.m. Arrangements for large groups.

Storage capacity: 3,000,000 gallons.

Directions: I-94 to Paw Paw exit 60. Look for the "Cask Wine" Tower.

Warner is the biggest winery in Michigan, possibly the busiest. The company is moving in several directions to build a reputation for premium quality. Warner takes pride in its vintage-dated varietal wines.

At the helm is James J. Warner, third generation chief of a family business begun by his grandfather, John Turner, in 1938. Turner, a grape broker and supplier of equipment, fell naturally into winemaking. In 1951, his son-in-law, James K. Warner, was made president of Turner's Michigan Wineries, though Turner remained active until his death, in 1964.

James K. Warner turned over the reins to son Jim in 1976, remaining as chairman of the board of Warner Vineyards, Inc. The name change was made in 1973.

That year was significant for the Warner family and Warner Vineyards in other ways. It was the year the company won the Agricultural Development of the Year Award in Michigan for its Warner Brut Champagne, made by the French *méthode champenoise*. The grapes used for this exceptional dry sparkling wine were aurora, niagara, and delaware. Warner had begun planting French-American hybrid grapes in the mid-sixties, so the presence of the aurora in the blend was not surprising. For the Bicentennial Year's champagne, made in 1974, no native grapes (such as niagara and delaware) were used. Seyval blanc joined aurora in the blend, and the wine, priced at $10 a bottle, was aged two years.*

It is noteworthy that the Warner champagne, which won the award in 1973, had been made by Nathan Stackhouse, who by the time of its debut was making wines for Warner's next door neighbor, St. Julian. He is now with Leelanau Wine Cellars.

Warner has a secondary line under the Cask label, which includes generic wines and a series of charmat process, bulk-fermented sparkling wines known as Cask Imperial.

This is one of the really charming wineries to visit. The Paw Paw River flows through its front yard. You cross a small foot bridge to the visitors center and tasting room which is known as Ye Olde Wine Haus. There is also a 1912 Grand Trunk Railroad car on the property for visitor orientation. It is boldly lettered "Cask Imperial Line."

---

* The Taylor Wine Company of Hammondsport, New York sold a ten-year-old Bicentennial champagne for $75. It was 100% aurora.

Wines of Warner

Cask Line red and white wines include Cask Imperial Brut Champagne (bulk or charmat process) and other sparkling wines, and generic types of still wines such as chablis and burgundy. Still wine, around $2.00; sparkling, around $3.00

Warner Michigan Brut Champagne: Aurora, niagara, and delaware grapes; French *méthode champenoise*. About $9.00.

Warner Michigan Light Solera Cream Sherry (around $4.00).

Warner Michigan Light Solera Port (around $4.00).

WHITE WINE

Aurora Blanc, some residual sweetness.
Liebestrauben, a sweet delaware.
Seyval Blanc, crisp, dry.

RED WINE

Baco Noir, brisk, light red.
Chancellor Noir, dark, heavy-bodied.
Chelois, full-bodied.
Maréchal Foch, dark, "biting," ages well.
Petite Rosé, blended red and white wines.

Price of wines: $3.00-$3.50.

Lake Sylvia Vineyard
red table wine

This robust dry red wine is a
first for Minnesota. It was made
from a unique blend of premium wine grapes, 54% Minnesota grown, 31% from New
York State, and 15% from California. Lake Sylvia Vineyard
red table wine is made in limited quantities by traditional
European methods and aged in
small oak barrels. It is an excellent accompaniment to many
hearty dishes and is best served at cool room temperatures.

David Macqueyt

Contents 4/5 Quart
Produced and bottled by Lake Sylvia
Vineyard at Maple Lake, Minnesota

The Wines
of Minnesota

"In days of old when knights were bold. . ."

There are still bold knights, and they live in Minnesota where winters bring temperatures of thirty degrees below zero. This is hardly a favorable climate for the survival of wine grapes. Yet there's a determined bunch of modern knights who believe they can meet the big challenge of winter survival in wine grapes, as well as two other challenges of almost equal importance: healthy, disease-resistant vines, and wine that really tastes good.

"Researchers have already met and overcome these three challenges," says David Bailly, whose wines made their debut in the spring of 1978. "But not in the same vine!" he adds. That is the crucial challenge. If it isn't met, Minnesota can be scratched as a wine-producing state, despite its favorable growing season.

The determined grape breeders who are pledged to meet that final challenge include Elmer Swenson of the Horticultural Research Center of the University of Minnesota's College of Agriculture. He has developed hundreds of crosses and given his best ones to the university. Others are Patrick Pierquet, research assistant in the Department of Horticultural Science and Landscape Architecture of which the research center is a part; David Macgregor, whose Lake Sylvia Vineyard was bonded late in 1976; and Thomas Fruth, a wine salesman with more than ordinary interest in the origins of the product he sells.

Pierquet is screening the Swenson varieties for the crosses which will

81

make the best wine. In addition, he is screening the various clones of local wild *riparia* grapes for both vine and wine quality.

Bailly's and Macgregor's wineries are not the first wineries to be bonded in Minnesota, but they're the first to make wines with Minnesota-grown grapes. At the end of Prohibition, a winery popped up in St. Paul, but the Old Sibley House label garnished wine made from grapes shipped in from other states. That winery went out of business in 1949. Then there was another winery licensed in 1972 at Stillwater, whose proprietor intended to sell wines from concentrates, but failed to produce any commercial wine.

The Minnesota Grape Growers Association, founded in 1975, has twenty-two members, most with vineyards of less than half an acre on which they experimentally grow such hybrids as aurora, foch, and baco noir. Wineacres, near Rush City and owned by Richard Williams, is of commercial size. So is the seven-acre vineyard owned by Gerald, Alma, and Perry Eisert, located south of Hastings. The Eiserts have planted an acre of vinifera, as well as seyval blanc, de Chaunac, Swenson 439 and Leon Millot, and a Russian grape called *rkatsiteli*, from which the Concannons in California make wine.

The Eiserts use Elmer Swenson's method of training vine trunks laterally, the better to mulch them against winter's bitter cold. They have invented a machine to roll and unroll bird netting over the vineyard.

If Minnesota cannot produce good, non-foxy wine, it won't be for lack of trying!

Some interesting cheeses are made in Minnesota to accompany the state's new wines. One is the excellent Treasure Cave Blue Cheese made near Faribault and aged in caves on the bluffs of the Straight River, on the site of an old brewery.

Swift and Company acquired Treasure Cave in 1966, straightened the Straight River, which really was crooked, and landscaped both banks.

Alexis Bailly Vineyard, Inc.

ESTABLISHED 1976

18200 Kirby Ave., Hastings, MN 55033

Phone 612-437-1413

Owner, David A. Bailly, sons and daughters.

Vineyard: 20 acres.

Visiting: Tuesday through Saturday, May through November, 10:00 a.m.-5:00 p.m. Closed in winter. Tours by appointment.

Storage capacity: 5,000 gallons.

Directions: 3 miles south of Hastings, 1 mile west of U.S. 61.

Alexis Bailly, after whom David Bailly's vineyard was named, is not his father. He was an infamous French trader, Bailly says, who came to Minnesota in the 1820's and, for selling watered-down whiskey to the Indians, in 1834, was run out of the territory. He later returned to the state and founded the town of Hastings. That hardly rules out ancestorship. David Bailly is a Minneapolis attorney.

The Baillys have six children; this is a family winery. The whole concept, Bailly explains, is to use Minnesota agricultural products. The winery is basically a log cabin made of Minnesota northern pine and white pine logs, with a foundation of local flagstone.

"People walk in among the barrels and vats and taste the wines there, and get the feel of a winery. There'll be no steel or fiberglass," Bailly says. Redwood tanks are used for fermentation, and small oak barrels for aging. He likes wood; all equipment that can be made of wood *is* made of wood.

Bailly has thoroughly researched his project, hunting out records of winter-hardy grape hybrids developed in France, working with the Minnesota experts and with his own vines.

The motto lettered over the vineyard name in the sign posted at the winery is "Where the grapes can suffer." This phrase is from remarks purportedly made by Baron Philippe de Rothschild, French proprietor of Chateau Mouton-Rothschild, in discussing California wines. California wines can never be great, the baron is reported to have said, because the vine is not challenged sufficiently in the temperate climate. "Grapes must suffer," were his words. (The baron may have modified this opinion in view of his now active interest in California's wine industry.)

Daughter Nan Bailly is the full-time manager of the winery and hostess to visitors.

Wines of Alexis Bailly

WHITE WINE

Country White (apple-grape).
Seyval Blanc

RED WINE

Country Red (riparia wild grapes).
De Chaunac
Leon Millot
Maréchal Foch

Price of Wines: $3.50-$5.00.

Lake Sylvia Vineyard
ESTABLISHED 1976

South Haven, MN 55382

Phone: 612-236-7743

Owner, David Macgregor.

Vineyard: 7 acres French hybrids, Minnesota and Macgregor hybrids, and vinifera (200 vines).

Storage capacity: 5,000 gallons.

Visiting: By appointment only.

Directions: Given to those who have appointments. It is not far from Minneapolis.

David Macgregor lives on Lake Sylvia where he works on new hybrid vines of his own and plants some of Elmer Swenson's most successful grapes. He also has small plantings of vinifera, including gewürztraminer and cabernet sauvignon.

The two wines which Macgregor makes are called simply Red Table Wine and White Table Wine.

"I'm interested in unique wines with regional character yet within the scope of traditional dry table wines," Macgregor says. "I accomplish this by blending in a small portion of wild *riparia* grapes with French hybrids and vinifera."

Riparia grapes give wine a slightly herbaceous flavor. When ameliorated to reduce the high acidity, such wine is much more like a vinifera *vin ordinaire* than a foxy labrusca, David Macgregor believes. The label on his red wine thus describes the contents: "This robust dry wine is a first for Minnesota. It was made from a unique blend of premium wine grapes, fifty-four per cent Minnesota grown, thirty-one per cent from New York State, and fifteen per cent from California."

Macgregor's winemaking is traditional European, and his wines are aged in small oak. He believes that the charm of wine is in its great diversity, and intends to stay "small scale and experimental," he says, until the "ideal" combination of varieties, cultural practices, and winemaking techniques result in the best wine he can make. Macgregor has been growing vines and experimenting since 1968, so he is far from an amateur. That in itself casts a rosy glow on the horizon of Minnesota winemaking.

Wines of Lake Sylvia Vineyard

Lake Sylvia Vineyard White, dry table wine.
Lake Sylvia Vineyard Red, dry table wine.
Baco Noir

Price of wines: Around $4.00.

MISSOURI TABLE WINE

hilltop, with the largest series of arched
opes, the historic Stone Hill Winery
ed by some of the finest vineyard
classic hillside vineyards
Hill began to make fine
w to be the second
nes of that day
d graced fine
his magnif-
past, is
ouri

Stone Hill

A dry red dinner wine made from the Münch grape, which
was developed in 1888 by Thomas Volnay Munson, and
named for the founder of Mount Pleasant.

MÜNCH

Missouri
Dry Red
Dinner Wine

Vintage 1978
•
Light Wine

MISSOURI

1978

Mount Pleasant

AUGUSTA, MISSOURI
LEON MILLOT

MISSOURI

LIGHT WINE
ESTATE BOTTLED BY
Mount Pleasant Vineyards
AUGUSTA, MISSOURI

MIDI

Wright County
Missouri
Johannisberger
Riesling

Table Wine
Produced and Bottled at the Winery by
MIDI Vineyard Ltd.
Lone Jack, Missouri

The Wines
of Missouri

Even though Missouri once was America's second-largest wine-producing state (after New York), she has been slow to shake off the restraints imposed by the temperance movement and Prohibition. However, in 1978 and 1979 grape-wine fever "busted out all over." Led by Lucian Dressel of Mount Pleasant Vineyards, and Clayton Byers of Montelle Vineyards and a few other earnest growers and winemakers, Missouri set out to reclaim her heritage.

A wine industry task force reported to Governor Joe Teasdale in late 1979 that Missouri could double production by 1985, and could become one of the top five wine-producing states within twenty years.

The task force pointed out the benefits of a state-supported wine industry: more revenue for the state; more jobs for its people; the development of currently non-productive land for vineyards; attraction of agricultural and industrial investment, and an increase in tourism.

Not only did the task force's cheerful report stir action, but another development focused the eyes of the nation on Missouri, specifically Augusta and environs. Augusta's leadership was ready when the federal Bureau of Alcohol, Tobacco and Firearms (BATF) called for petitions requesting designation of specific areas as American wine districts, and so Augusta became the first district to be so designated. This had nothing to do with alphabetical placement, much to do with historical perspective.

Persuasive evidence for the designation included proof that in the 1830s, when California was still a part of Mexico, vineyards were cultivated along the north banks of the Missouri River in the Augusta region, and that, in the last century, eleven wineries were active in the region. Though only two existed in the 1970s (Dressel's and Clayton Byers's Montelle Vineyards), there was, and is, in the new district, room for more.

The winemaking experiments conducted by Dr. Gary Bertrand, Department of Chemistry, University of Missouri-Rolla, and the experimental vineyards program being directed by Dr. Arthur Gaus, University of Missouri-Columbia, are part of the state's support program for its wine industry. Both men were on the task force. Bertrand, who studied enology at University of California-Davis, heads a study of fermentation methods as they apply to particular grape varieties, while Gaus's program involves selection and cultivation of grape varieties adapted to Missouri growing conditions.

Among those with firm plans for a Missouri winery are partners Dr. Jean R. Dupont, Sikeston surgeon, and Handy Moore, farmer with one hundred acres of catawba vineyard. Dr. Dupont is planting half of his own eighty acres to hybrid red wine grapes such as Foch, chancellor, and villard noir, and to hybrid white varieties including vidal and villard blanc. He also is planting a single vinifera variety, gewürztraminer for white wine; he believes that the Mississippi River Valley may be favorable for that classical grape of Alsace because of a similar winter climate. The Dupont winery is expected to open sometime between 1983 and 1985.

Another physician, Dr. Paul Levine, geneticist on the faculty of the Washington University School of Medicine, St. Louis, and grower-partner Robert O'Connor, hope to have phase one of their St. Clair Vineyards Winery operating early in 1981. Phase one is a 5,000 gallon winery housed in a small existing building. Phase two calls for expansion of facilities and capacity of 12,000 gallons, and phase three, if the men are successful, will move the winery into even bigger production. French hybrids are being planted on two pieces of land the men own (more than 100 acres), one above the Meramec River, the other overlooking Indian Creek, both at 700 feet altitude. The soils are totally different, but both have good air flow, says Dr. Levine. Until their vineyards are in full production, Dr. Levine and Bob O'Connor will buy grapes from William Stoltz of St. James, who has closed his winery, founded in 1968, but remains a grower.

The Firestone family may soon be as famous for wine as for tires. Albert Firestone, who describes himself as a gentleman farmer, may open his expansive and beautiful chateau winery near Dutzow, Missouri in the fall of 1981. A distant cousin, Brooks Firestone, already is a well-respected producer of California wines at the Firestone Vineyard, Los Olivos. Albert Firestone began planting his Stone Ledge Farm to French hybrids in 1975. A psychologist, Firestone has other interests in Ft. Lauderdale, Florida, but now spends most of his time at Stone Ledge and tells us he plans to market six Missouri wines.

Missouri has lost one winery, the Ziegler Winery at Cuba. The Lawrence Zieglers will have sweet and dry concord wines to sell until mid-1982, however.

Missouri Wine Tours

Missouri wineries tend to cluster, so it's easy to visit half a dozen or more in one trip. Take several leisurely days and you can reach most of them.

Begin with Bardenheier's in St. Louis, and then head westward toward Kansas City or southwest toward Springfield, stopping in the St. James-Rolla area to visit the Ashby-Rosati, Carver, St. James, Heinrichshaus, Peaceful Bend, and Reis wineries.

If you take the northern route toward Kansas City, you'll reach Augusta first on the meandering Missouri. There you may visit Mount Pleasant, Montelle, see Stone Ledge at Dutzow, then move on to Hermann (Stone Hill, Hermannhof, Bias) and to Portland (Green Valley).

Now, if you are really going to Kansas City, you'll head west on I-70 and can catch Kruger at Arrow Rock (Nelson), make a cheese stop at Emma, visit Bristle Ridge at Montserrat, and just before arriving in Kansas City, drop down to Lone Jack to find Midi Vineyards.

If you don't go to Kansas City, you can visit the St. James-Rolla wineries by dropping back to Hermann, taking Route 19 south to Steelville and Peaceful Bend, then backtrack the eight or nine miles to I-44 and the other area wineries mentioned earlier.

A good road map and the "Directions" under individual winery entries in this book will make the route clear. You may even be able to include the two rather isolated wineries, Bowman, on the Missouri at the Missouri-Kansas border (north of Leavenworth, Kansas), and Ozark, south of Springfield.

Ashby Vineyards, Inc.
ESTABLISHED AS ROSATI WINERY, 1934

Rt. 1 Box 55, St. James, MO 65559.

Phone: 314-265-8629

President, general manager, winemaker, Robert Ashby; secretary, Sally Ashby; vineyard manager, Hank Ashby; bookkeeper, Sarah Ashby.

Vineyards: 70 acres native grapes and hybrids.

Visiting: 9:00 a.m.-5:00 p.m. daily, November 1-May 1; Sunday, noon-6:00 p.m. May 1-November 1, 8:00 a.m.-6:00 p.m. Monday through Thursday; 8:00 a.m.-7:00 p.m. Friday, Saturday. Noon-6:00 p.m. Sunday.

Picnic Area: Patio with grape arbor.

Storage capacity: 75,580 gallons.

Directions: From St. James, Exit I-44 onto Highway 68. Go about ¼ mile south on 68 to 4-way stop. Left 5 miles. There are signs.

The Ashby family bought the old Rosati Winery* in 1972 and made their first wine that year. Grapes had been growing in the Rosati vineyards since shortly after the end of Prohibition. The winery was built in 1934 as a grape-growers' cooperative. The original building burned in 1969, and was rebuilt by the Ashbys when they took over the winery.

The Ashbys have nine children. The eldest, Hank, and his sister, Sarah, are involved in the winery. Within a few years the Ashbys hope to have well-developed champagne (French method) business. They plan to market demi-sec, dry, extra dry and pink champagne, sparkling Burgundy and sparkling Catawba when under full steam. Production of sparkling wines is now limited.

* Named for the town, which was named for Archbishop Joseph Rosati.

Wines of Ashby Vineyards and Rosati

Apple wine, spice wine, sangria, sparkling wines.

WHITE WINE

Chablis
Missouri Riesling
Dolce Bianco
Catawba
White Concord

RED WINE

Burgundy
Old Fashioned Concord
Chelois
Red Dinner Wine
Red Burgundy
Rosette, hybrid pink.
Dry Rosé
Vin Rosé, sweeter.

Price of wines: $2.25-$3.25 for table wines.

Bardenheier's Wine Cellars

ESTABLISHED 1873

1019 Skinker Parkway, St. Louis, MO 63112

Phone: 314-862-1400

President, John E. Bardenheier; executive vice-president-treasurer, Joseph A. Bardenheier; vice president-secretary, George E. Bardenheier; vice-president, Carl C. Bardenheier; chief winemaker, Carl B. Bardenheier; assistant winemaker, Ed Le May.

Vineyards: 75 acres French hybrids; many grape varieties purchased.

Visiting: Daily 9:00 a.m.-4:30 p.m. all year. Saturday 10:00 a.m.-4:00 p.m. Closed Sunday. General tours at 10:00 a.m. and 2:00 p.m. Special tours by appointment. Hospitality room, wine-tastings. Catered dinner parties.

Gift shop: Glasses, wine books, wine-related items.

Storage capacity: 850,000 gallons.

Directions: Winery is in the city.

Caught in urban sprawl, Big Bardenheier's covers a city block and makes a great many wines, from fresh grapes, juices, and concentrates. This old family winery makes both old-time wines and new wines from Missouri-grown grapes. Newcomers are from French hybrid vines planted by the Bardenheiers and a partner-grower at Koshkonong, in southern Missouri near the Arkansas border. From among thirty-five varieties planted experimentally, wines now on the market include several varietals that have won prizes.

Bardenheier's started life at the foot of the beautiful arch that loops over the city—though the arch was not there in 1873 when the first Bardenheier set up shop as a wholesale liquor distributor. The first Joseph Bardenheier came from Germany in 1865.

The firm finds mid-country location an advantage, George Bardenheier says. Supplies come from many sources—concentrated juices from Holland, Switzerland, and Yugoslavia, giant glass containers of wine from California, fresh grapes from Michigan as well as Missouri. The midwestern distribution is good. Bardenheier's covers a thirty-five state area.

There are good international markets for certain wines, and for Bardenheier's Catawba Grape Juice which goes to Hong Kong and Saudi Arabia.

Wines of Bardenheier's

Sparkling wines, sherries, ports, vermouth, fruit wines, cider. Bulk wines.

WHITE WINE

Sweet Catawba
Niagara
Sauterne
Country White, Missouri grapes.

RED WINE

Burgundy
Vino Rosso
Pink Catawba
Crackling Rosé
Country Pink, Missouri grapes.
Country Red, Missouri grapes.
Baco Noir
Chancellor
Chelois
Old Fashioned Concord
Many other wines

Price of wines: $1.75-$3.25.

Bias Vineyards and Winery
ESTABLISHED 1980

Route 1, Berger, MO. 63014

Phone: (home) 314-834-5475

Owner-winemaker, James Bias.

Vineyards: 5 acres catawba in production. Planting French hybrids.

Visiting: Phone for information.

Storage capacity: 3,000 gallons (expected).

Directions: 7 miles east of Hermann.

When we talked with the Biases, they didn't have their first wines in the bottle yet, but already the winery had expanded to take all the space in their 42-by-54-foot barn. They had intended to use only a third of the space. Activities were underway, but it was too early to tell much more than that the first Bias wine, catawba, would soon be available at something like $3.50 a bottle.

Bowman Wine Cellars
ESTABLISHED 1976

500 Welt St., Weston, MO 64098

Phone: 816-386-5235

Owner, Patrick O'Malley; winemaker, Elbert M. Pirtle.

Vineyards: 13 acres French hybrids.

Visiting: 8:30 a.m.-6:00 p.m. 7 days a week. Closed January.

Gift shop: Crystal and less expensive glasses, wine sets, cheeseboards, baskets, pewter, corkscrews, wine racks, Missouri sausage.

Restaurant hours: 11:30 a.m.-3:00 p.m. daily. Dinners Friday, Saturday, beginning at 7:30 p.m.

Storage capacity: 14,000 gallons.

Directions: Weston is easily reached from Kansas City or Leavenworth, Kansas. The winery is in Weston, a block off Main Street, behind City Hall.

More than a hundred antebellum homes remain in Weston, an historic Mississippi River town, where an ancient brewery along with some of its caves have been turned into an attractive winery with gift shop and a restaurant called America Bowman Keeping Room. (Lunch of chicken, barbecued beef, ham quiche, or other fare for $3.75. Dinners of country ham, seafood, prime ribs, $8.95-$10.95.)

The old Royal Brewery which houses the winery was built in 1840. Its arched cellars are of brick and native limestone. The bottom cellar is fifty-five feet below ground level and has a twenty-foot arched ceiling.

The winery, cellars, shop, and restaurant occupy a city block. Proprietor O'Malley, formerly in the investment business in Kansas City, bought the property in 1978. Ronald and Elizabeth Moreland had established the winery earlier.

The vineyard is planted to seyve-villard, baco, chancellor, chelois, and other French hybrids.

Wines of Bowman Wine Cellars

Apple wine, mead (honey wine).

WHITE WINE

Dry White
Sweet White
Niagara

RED WINE

Claret (Baco).
Missouri Concord

Price of wines: $2.90-$4.50.

Bristle Ridge Winery
ESTABLISHED 1980

Montserrat, MO 65336 (mail address, Rt. 1 Knob Noster, MO. 65336)

Phone: 816-747-5713

Owners, Richard Phillips; winemaker, Edward Smith.

Vineyards: 25 acres native and French hybrid grapes.

Picnic grounds, patio, tasting room.

Visiting: Noon-6:00 p.m. daily and Sunday.

Storage capacity (projected): 300,000 gallons.

Directions: 4 miles east of Warrensberg on Highway 50.

Richard Phillips, an engineer, and Ed Smith, a farmer, made 2600 gallons of wine in the fall of 1980, their first year, but both men were planning to leave their other occupations by the time of their second harvest, to become full-time growers and winemakers. They look to a 70,000 gallon production in a few years, and are proud to be making dry wines from Missouri grapes, including catawba and true Missouri riesling from very old vines.

Bristle Ridge Winery is a three-story, vine covered building to which the men already were adding 60 by 20 feet of space halfway along to their '81 vintage.

Phillips, who made wines as an amateur for nine years, says he does not use traditional methods of fermentation. The men envision an active winery program including an annual fall festival.

Wines of Bristle Ridge Winery

WHITE WINE

Catawba, extra dry.
Seyval Blanc.

RED WINE

Catawba Rosé, dry.
De Chaunac Rosé, dry.

Other wines forthcoming.

Price of wines: $3.00-$4.00.

Carver Wine Cellar
ESTABLISHED 1979

P.O. Box 1316, Rolla, MO 65401

Phone: 314-364-4335

Owners, Laurence R. and Mary Carver.

Vineyards: 7 acres vinifera (70 percent) and hybrids (30 percent).

Visiting: No set hours; phone for times.

Storage capacity: 5,000 gallons.

Directions: Follow 63 south of Rolla 6 miles to state highway W. Right turn 1500 feet, right turn again at gravel road, 1500 feet.

Laurence Carver is a physicist and research engineer at the University of Missouri-Rolla. Mary, his wife, is a medical technologist at a local clinic. The Carvers manufactured vinegar for ten years in California, then decided they'd rather make wine. Carver says, "so we came back to our home state."

Having lived in California for so long, it was probably natural for Carver to plant his vineyards predominantly to vinifera varieties of grapes. He tells us that in some ways the classical grapes are easier to care for than the hybrids. When we talked with him, he was in the midst of bottling thirty-five wines, variations of wine made from fifteen kinds of grapes, from different vineyards. It was part of a research project for the state horticultural department, he said, mentioning that there are seven experimental plots in the state where extensive vineyard testing goes on.

Carver says that his primary interest is in quality, particularly from vinifera vines. The Carvers hope to build to a capacity of ten or fifteen thousand gallons. They built their winery themselves. There are five children in the family, three of whom are old enough to be helpful with the work in summer and on weekends.

Wines of Carver Wine Cellar

WHITE WINE

Chardonnay
White Riesling
Seyval Blanc

RED WINE

Baco Noir
Cabernet Sauvignon
Chancellor
Villard Noir

Price of Wines: Hybrid grape wines, $3.00-$3.50.
Vinifera grape wines $4.50-$5.00.

Green Valley Vineyards
ESTABLISHED 1973

Highway D, R.R., Portland, MO 65067

Phone: 314-676-5771

President and winemaker, Nicholas A. Lamb; vice-president, Margarette C. Lamb; vineyard manager, Nicholas C. Lamb.

Vineyards: 15 acres French hybrids.

Visiting: Daily 2:00 p.m.-5:00 p.m. or 6:00 p.m.; Saturday 10:00 a.m.-5:00 p.m.; closed Sunday.

Tours and tasting.

Storage capacity: 20,000 gallons.

Directions: I-70, off at Williamsburg, follow State Road D. Winery is 13 miles south of I-70, overlooking Missouri River to the mouth of the Gasconade River. There are signs to guide you.

"We like wines, and we used to enjoy Chateau Latour, but it got too high priced, so we decided to make our own," Nicholas Lamb comments.

Lamb, a chemical engineer who had been making wine on a small scale for years, knew about Philip Wagner's thirty-year success with French-American hybrid grapes. They are what he was thinking about, since the Lambs owned twenty acres of land used for hunting; it was just right for grapes.

He and Margarette have six sons. Two of them are involved in the winery operation. Lamb senior has retired from his professional career to devote full-time to the vineyards and winery. The grapes planted here are exclusively hybrids, most of them reds such as baco, chancellor, cascade, chelois, and Maréchal Foch. Most of the vines are now mature, so wine quality has improved since the first production in 1973, though there have been problems. Lamb doesn't make any claim to having reproduced Chateau Latour. He just says, "We'll play it by ear and if people like our wines we can produce more."

That people do like their wines is evidenced by the array of gold medals Green Valley wines have been winning at the Missouri State Fair, and by visitors who keep returning for wines they enjoy.

Wines of Green Valley

WHITE WINE

Chablis
Rhine
Catawba, from purchased grapes.
Green Valley White Grape Wine

RED WINE

Natural Burgundy
Natural Red
Green Valley
Red Grape Wine
Côte Sans Dessins, hybrid blend.
Chancellor
Chambourcin
Maréchal Foch
Others

Price of wines: $2.15-$4.40.

Heinrichshaus Vineyards and Winery
ESTABLISHED 1979

Rt. 2, Box 139, St. James, MO 65559

Phone: 314-527-4794

Owners, Heinrich and Lois Grohe.

Vineyards: 6 acres French hybrids and native grapes.

Visiting: 9:00 a.m.-6:00 p.m. daily June 10 through summer. Sunday noon-6:00 p.m. During school year, open only on weekends.

Picnic grounds; wine racks, corkscrews, etc.; pottery, local craftworks for sale; fresh grapes available in season.

Storage capacity: 2,000 gallons (to be expanded).

Directions: From St. James, south on 68 to the first and only traffic light; Left on KK (old route 66) to U, which dead ends. A winery sign directs you north 3 miles.

"Where I come from," says Heinrich Grohe, "if you drink a glass of water, people think you're sick!" Grohe is German and grew up in a land where drinking wine is as natural as eating. He came to America in the 1950's, and settled near St. Louis. Since he found the available wines not to his taste, he began making his own. The Grohes bought their St. James area property in 1966 and planted vines, including villard blanc, chelois, and de Chaunac. Some vines of the native type were already there, including catawba and the unique Missouri cynthiana (or Norton) red wine grape. There was also cascade, a hybrid that ripens in August and is good to eat, but doesn't make very good red wine in this part of Missouri, Grohe says.

Both Grohes work full time; he as an engineer, Lois as an art teacher. They have a teen-age daughter, Peggy, who is in school. For the present, winery hours must be fitted around the three busy schedules. Peggy, of course, spends much of her free time working at the winery. Her mother, as an artist, brings her skills into play for the benefit of the family enterprise, designing wine labels and signs.

Grohe says there's good fishing in the nearby Ozark streams, a tip to visiting fishermen.

Wines of Heinrichshaus

WHITE WINE

Prairie Blanc, a hybrid blend.
Vidal Blanc

RED WINE

De Chaunac
Landal

Price of wines: $2.75–$4.00.

Hermannhof Winery
ESTABLISHED 1978

330 East First St., Hermann, MO. 65041

Phone: 314-486-5959

Officers: President, James Dierberg; vice-president, Robert Kirchhofer; managing director, vineyard manager and winemaker, Guenther Heeb; chemist, Otto Klein.

Vineyards: 50 acres French hybrids planted spring of 1980.

Visiting: Winter 8:00 a.m.-5:00 p.m.; summer 9:00 a.m.-6:00 p.m.; Sunday 12-5:00 p.m. Guided tours ($1.00) include visiting 11 cellars. Special rates for groups.

Weinstube, outdoor wine garden, sausage and cheese shop, souvenirs, winemaking equipment.

Storage capacity: 30,000 gallons.

Directions: On Highway 100 East (First St.), Hermann.

Hermannhof winery, now registered as a national historical building, began life in 1847 as a brewery, and continued so until Prohibition. Renovated completely in the old style, the brewery has been turned into a winery with a shop that features eleven different kinds of homemade sausage as well as many imported and local cheeses.

Hermannhof has seating capacity for around seventy people to taste wines and munch sausage and cheese. The ancient cellars, like those of nearby Stone Hill, are a memorable sight to see.

Vineyards are planted to such grapes as seyval, vidal, and villard blanc, villard noir, rougeon, and chancellor. Until the vines produce, the winery will continue to buy both native and hybrid southern Missouri grapes, which will make wines of the kind Hermannhof plans to produce from its own crops.

"White Lady of Starkenburg" is Hermannhof's version of the popular German "Blue Nun" wine. Starkenburg is a town across the Missouri River; the brand will be the winery's main output.

Guenther Heeb, the major domo, tells us that Hermannhof intends to build to a capacity of fifty thousand gallons. Five thousand gallons were produced in 1979. Hermannhof participates in Hermann's *mai-fest*, sponsors an Oktoberfest and a sausage market as well as other festivals for the benefit of throngs of tourists who come every year to the historic town of Hermann on the Missouri.

Wines of Hermannhof Winery

WHITE WINE

White Lady of Starkenburg
Catawba
Missouri Riesling
Vidal Blanc

RED WINE

Chelois
Hunter's Choice
Settler's Pride

Price of Wines: $3.89.

Kruger's Winery
ESTABLISHED 1977

Arrow Rock, MO 65320

Phones: (Home) Harold Kruger 816-784-2325; Larry Kruger 816-761-4311

Owners, Harold and Larry Kruger.

Vineyards: 50-60 acres native grapes being planted; grapes purchased.

Visiting: Saturdays, Sundays, noon-6:00 p.m.

Storage capacity: 7,500 gallons.

Directions: 100 miles east of Kansas City, 175 miles west of St. Louis. From I-70, north on U.S. 65 to Marshall. From Marshall east on State 41 toward Arrow Rock State Park. Look for sign. Winery is on the left just before you come to the park.

According to the Krugers, Arrow Rock is a town "where you can step out of your car into the past." Many old buildings of the Civil War era and earlier are well preserved, for example the Old Tavern, built in 1834, where tourists may dine. Arrow Rock is the jumping off place for the Santa Fe Trail, Harold Kruger says. Among the famous men who lived here were Dr. John Sappington, who first used quinine to treat malaria, and the artist George Caleb Bingham, whose home is a national landmark. Bingham's paintings reflect the history and political climate of his day. They include "Fur Traders Descending the Missouri," "Daniel Boone Coming Through the Cumberland Gap," and "Stump Speaking."

Daniel Boone's sons made salt in this salt springs area, and Kit Carson lived across the Missouri River at Old Franklin. Arrow Rock has recently been the setting for the movie *Tom Sawyer*, and the television production of *Huck Finn*.

There's a summer theater at Arrow Rock, good camping at Arrow Rock State Park, an archeological dig at Van Meter State Park ten miles north of Marshall, and other attractions, not the least of which is Kruger's Winery.

Larry, a Kansas City postal supervisor, and Harold, a plant maintenance engineer, planned their vineyards and winery as Larry began thinking about a retirement career. They are planting about 4,000 vines a year, and will stop with fifty or sixty acres. All grape varieties being planted are native to Missouri. "They are easier to grow than the hybrids, less expensive, and a challenge to us in making good wines," says Harold. Missouri Riesling, concord, catawba, and niagara are the chosen varieties.

Both men have families to help with the farming and winemaking.

Wines of Kruger's

WHITE WINE

Missouri Riesling, made German-style.
Niagara, sweet, semi-sweet, and dry.

RED WINE

Concord, sweet, semi-sweet, and dry.
Pink Catawba, sweet, semi-sweet, and dry.

Price of Wines: $3.20-$3.60.

Midi Vineyards Ltd.
ESTABLISHED 1977

Rt. 1, Lone Jack, MO. 64070

Phone: 816-524-7760

Co-owners, president, Dutton Biggs; vice-president-winemaker, George Gale.

Vineyards: 10 acres French hybrids, some vinifera.

Visiting: 10:00 a.m.-6:00 p.m. daily; noon to 6:00 Sunday. Closed weekdays January and February.

Storage capacity: 7,000 gallons.

Directions: 2 miles east of Lone Jack, 1½ miles north on Hwy. 50 to Co. F.

When asked, "When did it become crystal clear that you wanted to operate a winery?" Dutton Biggs, a structural engineer (architect), laughed and replied, "I don't think that has happened yet!"

However, his partner, George Gale, Ph.D., has been up to his elbows in grapes and wine for many years. A philosophy professor at the University of Missouri in Kansas City, Gale describes his primary pursuit as "kind of abstract. You're using your head all the time. I had to get into something sticky and gooey!"

Gale emphasizes that Midi's vineyards, started in 1972, are still experimental. As many as 100 varieties of grapes are growing. Successes include two little-known grapes obtained from Davis (University of California), *cloeta* and *valerian*. Cloeta is a super-grape for red wine, Gale declares, not subject to phylloxera, and producing a good crop on Missouri soil. "Put a couple of vintages together and lay it up against a *nouveau* gamay and you'd think it was the same thing!"

Valerian "keeps coming through like a hard, flinty French Chablis," Gale reports. He wants to plant thirty or forty more vines and check the quality. He has been able to grow and make good wine from Johannisberg riesling. Botrytis occurs every year so that the wine has the characteristic German taste and style.

Gale said that, after he'd bought the entire six-gallon production of the vineyard's fifteen rayon d'or vines for himself and his wife, it dawned on him that a grape that made such a crisp, well-balanced, "really nice wine" should be recommended for the territory. The philosopher-winemaker believes that Leon Millot is the best red wine grape for the area.

He brought from Germany several vines that are being checked for disease resistance and cold-hardiness at Geneva, and is checking French research which he believes the wine community has missed. Gale is optimistic about the future of wine in Missouri, observing that while there still are some "hill-billy" wines being made in the state, winemakers are catching on fast. He regards Lucian Dressel (Mount Pleasant) as the leader in Missouri viticulture and thinks that Dressel is making the best wines.

Wines of Midi Vineyards

WHITE WINE

Johannisberg Riesling
Missouri Riesling
Seyval Blanc
Vidal Blanc
Villard Blanc

RED WINE

Baco Noir
Chancellor
Concord
Isabella
Leon Millot
Maréchal Foch
Sweet and Dry Rosé wines, hybrid blends.

Price of Wines: $3.20-$7.25 (J. Riesling).

Montelle Vineyards, Inc.
ESTABLISHED 1969

Rt. 1, Box 94, Augusta, MO 63332

Phone: 314-228-4464 (or 241-7500)

Owners, Clayton W. Byers and Nissel Byers; director of operations, Brian Byers; business manager, Robert Slifer.

Vineyards: 9 acres French hybrids and vinifera, a research vineyard. Other vineyards leased.

Visiting: Daily 11:00 a.m.-6:00 p.m. Sunday noon-6:00. Tours of the vineyard. Recreational hiking through woodlands and bird sanctuary.

Tasting room, picnic facilities, cheese with wine samples.

Storage capacity: 5,000 gallons.

Directions: Winery is on Augusta Bottom Road between town of Augusta and Washington. Go 3 miles from Mt. Pleasant winery on this road. Montelle is on a bluff overlooking the Missouri River. It is 45 miles from St. Louis.

Clayton Byers was struck with grape-and-wine fever, while listening to Alexis Lichine lecture during an Experiment in International Living program, back in 1963. The meeting was held at the Hotel Chase in St. Louis; attendees were liberally sampling great growths of Bordeaux wines.

Byers, a journalist, then read Alexis Lichine's *Wines of France* and took to visiting wine growing areas in many states, studying and analyzing the wines. He is quick to admit that his interest soon grew into an obsession.

He chose his vineyard site believing the area to have great potential for growing fine wine grapes. Byers says his aim is simply to produce the finest wines possible from Missouri-grown grapes.

Clayton and Nissel Byers have three sons, one of whom, Brian, has grape fever, too. He's director of operations and his mother is treasurer of Montelle Vineyards. She also teaches school.

The Byers family has nearly fifty varieties planted, and there'll be a winnowing of the best ones for wine, as they prove themselves. Meanwhile, Clayton blends wines to achieve the results he wants, sometimes as many as five varieties in one wine. White wines spend a year in wood, six months in bottle before they're sold. Red wines age one-and-one-half years in oak, a year in bottle.

Future plans call for a new winery, and the Byerses have had an architect study functional operations in Napa Valley. Byers considers

Robert Mondavi a model winemaker and believes that there's something to be learned about winery layout from such a master. The new winery will be beautified by the old-fashioned rose garden the Byers family takes pride in. Roses are Clayton Byers' *other* obsession.

Byers, formerly a newspaper writer and public relations man, has written a book, *The Wineries of Missouri* (New Sunrise Press, $12.00), with photographs by George C. Harris.

Wines of Montelle Vineyards

WHITE WINE

Miraclair White Premium Blend
Golden Miraclair, aurora with delaware.
Centennial Farm Catawba, semi-dry.
River Country White

RED WINE

Miraclair Red
Montelle's Miraclair Red Reserve
De Chaunac, semi-dry.
River Country Red
St. Wenceslas Wine, fruit extracts on baco noir base.

Price of wines: $3.39-$6.99 *(Montelle's Miraclair Red Reserve).*

Mount Pleasant Vineyards
ESTABLISHED 1881

Augusta, MO 63332

Phone: 314-228-4419

Owners, Lucian and Eva Dressel.

Other property, The Winery of the Abbey, Cuba, MO.

Vineyards: 25 acres native Missouri and French hybrid grapes.

Visiting: Daily 10:00 am.-5:30 p.m. Sunday noon-6:00 p.m.

Storage capacity: 60,000 gallons.

Directions: Highway 94, 30 miles from St. Louis.

Back in the last century, when Missouri was our country's second largest wine-producing state, there were eleven wineries in Augusta alone. Now there are two in this little village of German heritage. One is Mount Pleasant, founded nearly one hundred years ago by a Lutheran minister, Reverend Friedrich Münch. The other is Montelle, which opened in 1969.

Mount Pleasant is on a hilltop overlooking the Missouri River Valley. The river itself is about a mile away. Lucian and Eva Dressel were in their twenties when they bought Mount Pleasant in 1966, and began restoring it to its old function. During the dry years the winery had been used for storage, then for mushroom culture, and finally as an apartment house. There are underground cellars. A hump in the grassy lawn in front of the winery shows where one of them is.

Lucian Dressel, a graduate of Harvard College and Columbia Business School, owes his interest in grape culture to Philip Wagner, whose book *American Wines and Winegrowing* has inspired so many. Dressel sees no future for the vinifera grape in Missouri, although he cultivates several varieties experimentally. The Dressel wines are of French hybrid varieties and several native Missouri grapes, the Münch, which hybridizer Thomas Munson named after Mount Pleasant's founder, and the Cynthianna. Münch is little grown any more. Lucian Dressel believes himself to be the only grower, and takes pride in perpetuating a wine made of the founder's own grape. The grape is coal black, and if fast-pressed, yields white wine. But the Dressels make of it a staining purplish wine with its own taste.

The Cynthianna grape belongs to a vine family discovered in the Carolinas about 1800. It makes deep red wine with a taste resembling cranberries. Both Stone Hill and Wiederkehr in Arkansas make wine of Cynthiana also, spelling it with only one *n*. The grape is also known as Norton and Virginia seedling.

Dressel grew up in Granite City, Illinois, where his parents were processors of milk, making butter and ice cream. Winemaking is much the same thing, Dressel believes. "In both cases you are taking a liquid agricultural crop and keeping it from spoiling."

The 1976 harvest at Mount Pleasant was wonderful. The summer was long and warm and the grapes sweetened. Picking began in late August at a temperature of ninety degrees, and ended in a snowstorm on October 28. A quick freeze with grapes still on the vine enabled Lucian Dressel to try his hand at an ice wine. *Augustaner* '76 is not at all like a German *eiswein*, which usually is somewhat sweet. The wine is more like a vermouth, interesting as an apèritif with a twist of lemon.

In 1978, it happened again. Ice wine plus many new varietals including Emigré Blanc (100% villard) in three bottlings, one from each of Missouri's growing regions.

The Dressels have several suggestions for visitors to their area who are interested in good food as well as drink. Restaurant Femme Osage at Washington, Missouri, housed in a Civil War vintage residence on the Missouri River and presided over by its woman chef, Pat Langenberg, offers French Provincial-style menus. Dressel makes the restaurant's wines from the acre of vines owned by Roy and Pat Langenberg.

At St. Charles you'll find the St. Charles Vintage House and Wine Garden, which used to be the Wepprich Winery. The land on which the building stands was in a Spanish grant to Moutherin Bouvet in 1792. The building itself dates to 1860. In this Swiss chalet restaurant Mount Pleasant wines are featured, though not exclusively.

In the town of Augusta there's a marvelous bakery. Shirley Toedebusch makes sour dough hearth bread, honey wheat bread, brandied raisin bread, many other breads, pastries, and cookies. We've heard there's now another excellent bakery in Augusta, called "The Bread Shed."

Wines of Mount Pleasant Vineyards

WHITE WINE

Emigré Blanc (100 percent villard), dry.
Vidal Blanc, dry.
Delaware, dry.
Missouri Riesling
Niagara
White Labrusca

RED WINE

Chancellor, dry.
Chelois, dry.
Cynthianna

De Chaunac, dry.
Leon Millot, dry.
Red Labrusca
Red Concord
Münch
Emigré, *Florental*, and *Mount Pleasant Rosé* wines.

Price of Wines: $2.99–$4.99.

The Winery of the Abbey, Cuba, Mo.

A sales facility opened by the Dressels in the summer of 1980, this is not an abbey; it just looks like one. It is composed of a set of three buildings of Tennessee granite, connected with archways, which give it a medieval look. The Abbey is a pleasant wayside for travelers on Interstate 44. Cheese as well as wine is available. The wines at opening were half a dozen chosen from Mount Pleasant's cellars, but since Missouri law requires that such a facility must make its own wine, Lucian will turn the Abbey into a second full winery. He tells us that half the grapes for Mount Pleasant's wines come from the Cuba environs.

Carla Schnelt manages the Abbey sales. Her husband's family are growers.

Directions: Interstate 44, 6 miles west of Bourbon, Missouri, on UU. Right off the highway.

Ozark Vineyards
ESTABLISHED 1976

Chestnut Ridge, MO 65630

Phone: 417-587-3555

President, Hershel Gray; vice-president, Herschel Chudomelka; secretary-treasurer, Joe Lewis.

Vineyard: 20 acres native and hybrid grapes.

Visiting: Weekdays, 9:00 a.m.-7:00 p.m.; Sunday noon-6:00 p.m.

Salesroom has wineglasses, local cheese, Missouri ham.

Storage capacity: 20,000 gallons.

Directions: South of Springfield 30 miles at junction of state routes 176-West and 65. From Branson, 10 miles north. Turn in on 176-West, no access on 65.

Proximity to the big tourist town of Branson brings many visitors to Ozark Vineyards winery. Branson is Shepherd of the Hills country, famous for its lakes, Table Rock State Park, and as "Silver Dollar City."

Hershel Gray, a grape grower, and four businessmen friends had been talking for years about starting a winery. In 1976 they made their dream a reality. Before the winery itself was built, they had grapes to make their first wines. The winery was opened, in 1978, with a good selection of wines made from native grapes and hybrids.

Gray called upon a friend and experienced winemaker to produce these wines. He is none other than the proprietor of Stone Hill Wine Cellars at Hermann, James Held.

Wines of Ozark Vineyards

A sweet peach wine and non alcoholic catawba juice are specialties.

WHITE WINE

Aurora
White River White, semi-dry blend.
Niagara

RED WINE

Concord
Dry Red (Cascade).
Bonniebrook Rosé, semi-sweet.

Price of Wines: $2.59-$2.79.

Peaceful Bend Vineyard
ESTABLISHED 1972

Rt. 2, Box 131, Steelville, MO 65565

Phone: 314-775-2568

Owners and winemakers, Axel and Arne Arneson.

Vineyards: 20 acres French hybrids and vinifera (white riesling).

Visiting: Daily 10:00 a.m.-5:00 p.m. Closed Sunday. Tours can be arranged.

Storage capacity: 10,000 gallons.

Directions: On Highway M out of Steelville.

Axel Arneson, M.D., and Arne Arneson are father and son, Axel a gynecologist, Arne a broker. Their grape growing began as a hobby. When the vines produced more grapes than the two families could consume, the Arnesons began reading and experimenting with winemaking.

The Arneson women, Marilyn (Mrs. Axel, mother of Arne) and "Cookie" (Mrs. Arne) are also very much involved in the hobby that got a bit out of hand.

There have been four or five bad years. The 1976 crop yielded exactly 250 gallons.

In addition to their six acres courageously planted to riesling, the Arnesons grow baco noir, Leon Millot, and chancellor grapes, all French-American hybrids.

Peaceful Bend refers to the bend in the Meramec River where this vineyard is located. The wines are named for the Meramec and nearby towns of Huzzah (and Huzzah State Forest) and Courtois (elevation 1,223 feet). A few foothills away from Courtois in the Mark Twain National Forest area is a town named Enough. We do not expect the Arnesons to name a wine for it.

Wines of Peaceful Bend

All wines are hybrid blends.

Courtois, white
Meramec, red
Huzzah, rosé

Price of wines: $3.00-$3.50.

Reis Winery
ESTABLISHED 1979

Rt. 4, Box 133, Licking, MO 65542

Phone: (home) 314-674-3763

Owner, Val N. Reis.

Vineyards: 6 acres French hybrids (will be expanded).

Visiting: Friday, Saturday, Monday 10 a.m.-6 p.m. Sunday noon-6:00. Other times by arrangement.

Picnic facilities.

Storage capacity: 10,000 gallons.

Directions: 28 miles south of Rolla. Take US 63 to Junction CC; left (east) 4 miles to Maples Junction. There's a guiding sign at the 63-CC junction, by the filling station.

Val Reis (pronounced rice), his wife Joy and family lived in St. Louis, where they filled their back yard with sixty experimental vines. Neighbors thought them a bit loony, Reis admits, but every "wine and grape nut" understands.

The homegrown experiment helped to guide planting when the Reis family bought the present property, in 1972. But, there is a "problem." *All* of the French-American hybrids do well on the Missouri Ozark plateau, Val says, making it difficult to select those that will make the best wines. The elevation is 1,350 feet, the soil sandy clay; it is less rocky and somewhat more fertile than much of the rest of the area. The Reises grow grains, grasses, and soybeans, as well as grapes on their sixty-one acres.

Reis took an early interest in cultivating grapes, reading all the books he could find, notably those of Philip Wagner. "I used all of his suggestions," he tells us.

Val Reis still spends three days a week at his profession (chiropractor) in East St. Louis, Illinois, which explains the Friday through Monday winery hours.

Montauk State Park, of interest to campers and trout fishermen, is near the Reis Winery.

Wines of Reis Winery

WHITE WINE

Rhine, a dry blend.
Mountain White, a semi-sweet blend.
Seyval Blanc
Vidal Blanc
Villard Blanc

RED WINE

Burgundy, a dry blend.
Mountain Red, a semi-sweet blend.
Pink Catawba, from purchased grapes.
Leon Millot
Maples, blend of native and hybrid grapes.

Price of wines: $2.25-$5.00.

St. James Winery
ESTABLISHED 1970

Rt. 2, Box 98A, St. James, MO 65559

Phone: 314-265-7912

Owners, Jim and Patricia Hofherr.

Vineyards: 35 acres.

Visiting: 8:00 a.m.-6:00 p.m. daily. Sunday noon-6:00 p.m.

Sales shop: Cheese, glasses, wine books, as well as wine.

Storage capacity: 45,000 gallons.

Directions: I-44 to St. James turnoff. Right turn at the north access road B—back 3 blocks.

Jim Hofherr was a microbiologist, with an advanced degree from the University of Oklahoma, when he and his wife Patricia decided that they wanted to go into the wine business. They grow all their own grapes. Now they have thirty-five acres planted in traditional Missouri and Midwestern native varieties and the French hybrids.

The winery, which the Hofherrs built in 1970, is so constructed that visitors may guide themselves on tours by following the signs. This is certainly simpler than having to hire guides, or stop work and show visitors around. It is becoming a fairly frequent practice, but requires a layout that permits a good overview of the winemaking process.

The Hofherrs have four children who help with vineyard and winery work—and that's a super idea for anyone in the wine business!

Wines of St. James Winery

Fruit wines: Apple, blackberry, strawberry. Mead (honey wine).
Sparkling Wines: Dry champagne, pink catawba, cold duck (concord).

WHITE WINE

Niagara
Sweet Catawba
Velvet White
Vidal Blanc
Villard Blanc

RED WINE

Baco Noir
Cascade
Chelois
Cynthiana
Isabella
Mellow Red
Munson (limited).

Velvet Red
Villard Noir
Pink Catawba
Rosé

Price of Wines: $1.95-$2.75. Sparkling wines: $4.75.

Stone Hill Wine Company, Inc.
ESTABLISHED 1847

Rt. 1, Box 26, Hermann, MO 65041

Phone: 314-486-2221

President, treasurer, general manager, L. James Held; vice-president and secretary, Betty Ann Held; winemaker, David Johnson; restaurant manager, Gary Buckler.

Vineyard: 50 acres. New plantings of French hybrids in 1979.

Visiting: Daily 8:00 a.m.-5:00 p.m.; Sunday 12:00 noon-5:00 p.m. (later in summer). Charge of $1.00 for tour.

Restaurant hours: 11:00 a.m.-10:00 p.m. In winter, open weekends only.

Storage capacity: 110,000 gallons.

Directions: I-70, exit Highway 19 (south) to Hermann. Watch for signs.

Stone Hill, a beautiful winery to visit, became a National Historic District in 1969. The designation includes the winery, the old limestone cellars beneath it, and the grounds.

Stone Hill was founded by a German immigrant, Michael Poeschel, in 1847, and grew to be one of the largest wineries in the world—third largest, in fact, says Betty Ann Held. In the late 1800's, and early 1900's there were many wineries in Hermann. Their vineyards covered the hills. Stone Hill produced 1,250,000 gallons of wine in a year's time!

James and Betty Ann Held bought the historic property in 1965, and began restoring it. For forty years, during and after Prohibition, its arched limestone cellars, two stories deep, with water streaming down the stairs from the upper level, had been used for mushroom cultivation. The Helds phased out the mushrooms, not because they needed all that cellar space, but because of labor problems.

It wasn't only Prohibition that killed the wine industry in Hermann. The early settlers of the town were German, and its culture was German. As World War I approached, the growing anti-German feeling had many destructive effects. When Prohibition arrived, the owners of the Stone Hill Wine Company ordered their vineyards destroyed and equipment was either destroyed or given away.

The Helds hope some day to retrieve a set of twelve hand-carved "Apostle" casks which were sent to Germany at the time. They have acquired a single cask of the three that were given to the Stanislaus Seminary, and it is a part of Stone Hill's mini-museum. Jim and Betty Ann don't like to think about the beautiful old casks that were burned as firewood.

The $1.00 charge for a tour of this unique winery goes into a fund for restoring and maintaining the old buildings, which include a horse barn, now a crafts shop. Horses were once used to pull the delivery wagons filled with barrels of wine.

The Helds keep much Missouri tradition in their vines and wines. They are proud of their Norton wine because it is the child of cuttings of a half-acre—*all* that was left—of the old vineyards. This grape is also called Cynthiana and several wineries retain that old name for the wine.

Vintage 1847 Restaurant was opened at Stone Hill in 1979. Traditional German dishes are a specialty. Black Forest cake is a favorite dessert. Lunches are $2.50 to $4.75; dinners $8.00 to $10.75.

Stone Hill and its town, Hermann, are well worth a trip. The Helds, who sent a son and a daughter to study enology in California, are welcoming hosts who will tell you the whole story. There is a Maifest every year to help restore the old German culture. That may or may not be the time to visit. It brings crowds of tourists, so if you enjoy crowds, you'll love it.

Wines of Stone Hill Wine Cellars

Sparkling wine, bottle fermented.

WHITE WINE

Dry Catawba
Missouri Riesling
Golden Rhine (niagara).
Harvest Peach

RED WINE

Pink Catawba
Concord
Chelois
Montaigne Rouge (hybrid blend).
Montaigne Rosé (catawba).
Norton
Vin Rosé

Price of wines: $2.75-$3.50; Champagne $6.00.

The Wines
of Ohio

"The capacity of the Ohio valley . . . is practically illimitable. Already the mellow lines of Longfellow are not merely the poet's fancy, but literal truth:

> For the richest and best
> Is the wine of the West
> That grows by the Beautiful River.

"The next generation will see the choicest wines of the world made in California, Ohio, and Missouri. They will be exported to every foreign land. Americans will give them to their children, and use them freely in their households as our farmers do milk. . . ."

So wrote Albert D. Richardson in a book called *Beyond the Mississippi* in 1869. California comes closer to fulfilling the author's prophecy than either Ohio or Missouri. But Missouri caught fire in the late 1970s, determined to live up to her wine-producing potential. And Ohio blooms with more than thirty wineries.

Look at the geographic location of the state of Ohio and you will realize its advantages for winegrowing. Rolling terrain, not flat land, the better to expose grapes to the sun and provide good drainage. Lake Erie lies to the north to temper winter cold by giving up its stored summer heat; and the Ohio River borders that state on the south, its shores on both sides historically friendly to the vine.

Most wine people know something about the first Nicholas Longworth (1782-1863), who made sparkling catawba wine celebrated in verse by the poet Henry Wadsworth Longfellow. The wine was a great success in eastern restaurants, but the vines eventually fell victim to disease. The revival of winegrowing on the Ohio River and elsewhere in the state was late in coming, due for the most part to the temperance movement, Prohibition, and antiquated laws left over from those times. The average Ohioan isn't much of a wine drinker, either—Ohio ranking 37th among the states, drinking 1.06 gallons of wine a year. A Californian drinks 4.20 gallons.

Small wineries began to sprout throughout Ohio in the early 1970s, and the trend continues. A few have failed. Most of the new family wineries do not plan to expand much, and most find it practical to sell their products from the winery. Several combine winery and restaurant, which can be a great attraction for the public.

The state encourages the industry, and Ohio State University sponsors an annual Ohio Grape-Wine short course in which industry problems are scrutinized, problems such as frost damage, vine diseases, insect pests, and restraints on free enterprise.

Most Ohio winery owners belong to the Association of American Vintners and the Ohio Wine Producers Association. Through them, they reach their counterparts in other Midwestern states for mutually helpful discussions.

Bretz Winery
ESTABLISHED 1867

P.O. Box 17, Middle Bass, OH 43446

Phone: 419-285-2323

Owner, Leslie J. Bretz.

Vineyards: 25 acres, most native grapes, also hybrids. Sales room at rear of family home.

Visiting: All year, 8:00 a.m.-6:00 p.m. Closed Sunday.

Storage capacity: 10,000 gallons.

Directions: By plane or ferry boat from Sandusky.

Middle Bass Island is only a mile wide and three miles long, so it would be difficult to get lost there. Bretz Winery is more than 100 years old, and has remained a small family winery all that time. The oldest part of the winery was built in 1867, ten years after the Joseph Muellers and three other families bought the island. Three of the four founding families were related.

Leslie Bretz is a grandson of Joseph Mueller. Now in his eighties, Bretz and his sons Jim and Walter, still do nearly everything by hand, from planting the vines to picking the grapes, making the wine, bottling, and labeling it. They are sticklers for tradition and are proud to still be using three 160-gallon barrels, once used by Ohio's pioneer winemaker, Nicholas Longworth. The senior Bretz is known as a rugged individualist.

The wines these men make are traditional Ohio wines; there is something beautiful about that. Catawba was the famous wine of Longworth's day; the grape grows prolifically in the Lake Erie islands. The Bretzes make their wines primarily of catawba, concord, and delaware grapes. They have a devoted clientele and sell their wines not only on the island but ship to regular customers anywhere in Ohio.

The other winery on the island for years was Lonz, with its rather bizarre "chateau," which drew thousands of youthful revelers in George Lonz's later years and during subsequent management (Lonz died in 1969). The Lonz estate was purchased in 1979 by Meier's Wine Cellars.

Wines of Bretz

Bottle-fermented sparkling wines.
Concord juice.

WHITE WINE

Delaware, dry.
Sauterne, semi-sweet.

RED WINE

Claret, Concord base, dry.
Concord, semi-sweet.
Pink Catawba, semi-sweet.

Price of wines: About $2.00.

Brushcreek Vineyards
ESTABLISHED 1977

RR 4, 12351 Newkirk Lane, Peebles, OH 45660

Phone: 513-588-2618

Owners, Ralph A. and Laura Wise.

Vineyards: 10 acres.

Visiting: Daily except Sunday, 11:00 a.m.-8:00 p.m.

Amateur winemaking supplies.

Storage capacity: 2,000 gallons.

Directions: From Hillsboro, south on State 73 to Lowden (about 15 miles). Turn right on Elmville Road. Second road on right is Newkirk Lane. Brushcreek is at the end of the lane.

The Wises have five children who are in their teens and twenties. The entire family is involved in the winery operation. The winery is located in an old log building, built in 1820. That's one link to the past. Another is a family wine tradition. Ralph Wise's great-grandfather and his brother were proprietors of Kramer Wine Gardens at Dayton.

Ralph has been making wines for years—excellent wines, Mrs. Wise tells us. But he was a quality control engineer, not a professional winemaker, until a few years ago. Brushcreek Vineyards became a reality in 1973, when the Wise family bought the place.

The location is excellent, Ralph Wise believes, because it lies on the edge of the Ohio River Valley where the foothills of the Appalachians begin. Still, that beautiful territory is not free from peril—in 1978 two killing frosts wiped out the crop and the Wise family had to buy all of their grapes.

They grow both native and French hybrid varieties. Of the latter, aurora and villard blanc are the white grape varieties already planted. Chancellor, de Chaunac and Foch are the reds. Wise says he will probably plant more Foch, and he intends to plant catawba for rosé wine. Brushcreek, according to plan, will one day be a 10,000 gallon winery.

Wines of Brushcreek Vineyards

WHITE WINE

Dry White Wine
Niagara, semi-sweet.

RED WINE

Chancellor, dry.
Dry Red Wine
Sweet Catawba Rosé
Concord, semi-sweet.
Highland Fling, a sweet blend.

Price of wines: $3.25-$3.75.

Buccia Vineyards
ESTABLISHED 1978

518 Gore Road, Conneaut, OH 44030

Phone: 216-593-5976

Owner, Alfred J. Bucci.

Vineyard: 5 acres.

Visiting: Fridays 4:00 p.m.-8:00 p.m., Saturdays 2:00 p.m.-7:00 p.m. all year. Other times by appointment.

Storage capacity: 1,200 gallons.

Directions: From Interstate 90 exit State Rd. 7 North to US-20. West on US-20 3 miles to Gore Rd. North about 2 miles.

Alfred and Joanna Bucci planted their vineyard in 1975. Bucci's grand-father had planted concords in Ashtabula County, in 1908, and made wine of them for family use. So, Alfred was following a family tradition. He grows some concord, but most of the Bucci wines are made from French hybrids, which do well in the vineyard.

Buccia Vineyards are part of a cluster of Lake Erie wineries that might be visited in one day. Markko is close by, Grand River and Chalet Debonné aren't far, either, and then, with reservations, you might be able to scoot into Cleveland Heights, have dinner at Au Provence, and taste the wines of the Cedar Hill Wine Company.

Wines of Buccia Vineyards

WHITE WINE

Aurora
Seyval Blanc
Steuben

RED WINE

Baco Noir
Chelois
Concord

Price of wines: $3.00-$4.00.

Catawba Island Wine Company
(Mon Ami Champagne Company)
ESTABLISHED 1934

326 West Catawba Road, Catawba Island, Port Clinton, OH 43452

Phone: 419-797-4445

President, Robert Gottesman; winemaker, Archie Stinson.

Vineyards: None; grapes purchased on contract.

Restaurant in winery.

Visiting: Noon (11:30 a.m. in summer)-10:00 p.m. Sales, no tastings or tours.

Storage capacity: 100,000 gallons.

Directions: On Highway 53, ½ mile north of intersection with Highway 163.

Norman Mantey, as president and sales manager of Mantey Vineyards, owned and operated this winery as well. Leon Adams, in his book *The Wines of America*, called him the busiest vintner in America. In addition to running two wineries, Norman Mantey also operated a restaurant at his Mon Ami Winery.

"With its picturesque vaulted underground cellar, the Mon Ami Winery could become a showplace for the wine industry of the Sandusky area if the proprietor didn't work at so hectic a pace. He has no time to show the vaults to visitors," Adams wrote.

Then the colorful Mr. Mantey sold both wineries to Meier's Wine Cellars in 1980 and retired to a less hectic life. Robert Gottesman is the new president.

Mon Ami Winery was built of limestone in 1872, by a grower cooperative, and was purchased in 1956 by Norman Mantey. The restaurant features steaks (sometimes including buffalo steak) and such appetizers as sauerkraut balls. Chardonnay and several wines from French hybrid grapes are available, as well as many time-honored wines from native Ohio grapes, to accompany dinner or to purchase and take home.

Wines of Mon Ami

Sparkling Wines
Port, Sherry

WHITE WINE

Pinot Chardonnay
Seyval Blanc
Dry and *Sweet Catawba*
Delaware
Niagara
Others

RED WINE

Foch Rouge
Sweet Concord
Pink Catawba
Rosé
Others

Price of wines: Most around $2.00-$2.50. Sparkling wine, $5.00.

Cedar Hill Wine Company
ESTABLISHED 1974

2195 Lee Road, Cleveland Heights, OH 44118

Phone: 216-321-9511

Owner, Au Provence Inc.; president, Dr. Thomas Wykoff; chef and vice-president, Richard Taylor; general manager, Mary Partin.

Vineyards: 1 acre; most grapes purchased from growers.

Retail store sells wines made on the premises and over 200 others. Hours: 12:00 p.m.-6:00 p.m. Tuesday-Saturday.

Winemaking supplies.

Visiting: At present limited to patrons of Au Provence Restaurant. Dinner hours: Monday-Friday 6:00 p.m.-9:45 p.m. Friday 6:00 p.m.-11:00 p.m. Saturday (two seatings) 6:30 p.m.-9:15 p.m. Reservations required.

Storage capacity: 4,500 gallons.

Directions: Follow your nose to fragrant Au Provence Restaurant in Cleveland Heights. Winery is below restaurant.

The story of Cedar Hill Wine Company is, first of all, the story of a tiny restaurant with superb cuisine, and of its dynamic proprietor, Dr. Thomas Wykoff, a surgeon in his mid-forties. Wykoff heads the ear, nose, and throat department of St. Luke's Hospital in Cleveland. His restaurant, which is mentioned frequently on "best places to eat" lists, is Au Provence. The skilled and ambitious young chef is Richard Taylor, now a full partner in the operation.

Wykoff works eighteen-hour days seven days a week and says he probably always will. He and Taylor teach a class in "Ma Cuisine,"* in the adult education program of a local high school, and often give food demonstrations at meetings of grape-growers and winemakers.

Wykoff's wine is called Chateau Lagniappe. His restaurant orientation came about as a result of practicing medicine for four years in New Orleans, and forming a friendship with famous restaurateur Al Pierce of Restaurant Bon Ton. "Much of Pierce's philosophy rubbed off on

---

* The name of a book by Auguste Escoffier, celebrated French chef (1846-1935).

me," says Wykoff. "I observed his love of people and the enjoyment he found in presenting superb food and wine to patrons who have become his friends."

By the time Dr. Wykoff left New Orleans, he could prepare creole dishes as well as any of the native chefs. He returned to Cleveland in 1970 and started making wines. In 1974, he found the beauty parlor which he turned into a French country-style restaurant with a Creole flair. It had to be rebuilt, and the winery came first. "Construction was done by a carpenter, a high school student, an electrician, and myself. We worked daily from 6:00 p.m. until 1:30 a.m., plus twenty hours on weekends," says Tom Wykoff. "I bought our first ton of grapes, Leon Millot (French hybrids), the day after receiving federal approval of the winery, September 24, 1974. We made approximately 1,500 gallons and opened the restaurant in February of 1975."

Chateau Lagniappe wines are made for the restaurant and are available to the public through several Cleveland outlets.

The doctor bought red wine grapes (chancellor, millot, and chambourcin) from ex-banker Bill Worthy, until Worthy needed them for his own Grand River Winery. Two other top-notch growers supply the white grapes. They are John Moorhead and Arnulf Esterer of Markko Vineyard . Wykoff makes his wines from vinifera and French grapes, blending varieties with skill.

Au Provence Restaurant patrons who have to wait for a table in the thirty-two place dining room above the winery are usually taken downstairs and allowed to sample from the barrel and munch cheese. Wykoff is very much the personable host, and as a dedicated winemaker also, he can make the wine sampling lecture so interesting that people sometimes argue about who has to leave the winery when a table becomes available upstairs.

Beverly Wykoff is a beautiful woman with a career of her own as a social worker. She is also a student of modern dance. The couple have three children.

Wines of Cedar Hill Wine Company
(Chateau Lagniappe label)

WHITE WINE

Champagne
Chardonnay
White Riesling

Vidal Blanc
Seyval Blanc
Delaware
Dutchess
Steuben
Wiemer's White Vinifera

RED WINE

Chambourcin
Leon Millot-Chancellor
Maréchal Foch
Maréchal Foch-Landot
Maréchal Foch-Nouveau

Price of Wines: In restaurant, $6.00 and up; less at retail outlets.

Chalet Debonné Vineyards
ESTABLISHED 1971

7743 Doty Road, Madison, OH 44057

Phone: 216-466-3485

President and winemaker, Anthony P. Debevc; vice-president and vineyard manager, Tony J. Debevc.

Vineyards: 40 acres.

Home winemaking supplies. Fresh juices at harvest.

Visiting: Tuesday-Saturday 1:00 p.m.-8:00 p.m.; Wednesday and Friday until midnight. Closed Sunday, Monday.

Snack foods available (cheese, sausage, homemade bread).

Storage capacity: 70,000 gallons.

Directions: I-90 east, Madison exit. South on 528. Cross Grand River bridge, the first road on left (Griswold) 2½ miles. Follow signs.

Chalet Debonné is a winery built to look like a Swiss chalet; it has a large tasting room, where people can sit at small tables covered with red-checkered tablecloths and buy snacking foods to go with the free samples of wine. It also has a patio and grape arbor for summer picnicking. The Debevcs have been discovered by visitors from nearly all of the fifty states, and from almost as many foreign countries. They'll welcome you warmly and show you how they make their wines. If you are lucky, you may meet all of the Debevcs, including eighty-seven year-old Grandpa.

Tony and Rose Marie, and Tony Jr., their son, and his wife Beth are all involved in the winery and vineyards, though Beth has less time since a small daughter's arrival. Tony has a degree in pomology from Ohio State; his father has always been a grape-grower. Winemaking comes naturally for all three generations.

The Debevcs built the chalet themselves and lined the tasting room with old barn boards. The winery is directly below the tasting room. Red wines are aged in fifty-gallon whiskey barrels in a new section, added in 1974. Since then the winery has been modernized.

Concord and niagara wines were the first varietals of Chalet Debonné, because these were the grapes the family had always grown. Nowadays, if you're going to be successful in marketing your own wines in the Midwest, you also need French-American hybrids. The Debevcs planted hybrids and an experimental plot of vinifera vines, difficult, but not impossible, to grow in the Midwest.

You can taste, nibble, buy wines or not, but you should know that the Debevcs like a little less informality in the evenings. There are little signs on the table requesting you not to come in jeans after eight o'clock. So if you come late, dress up a bit!

Wines of Chalet Debonné

WHITE WINE

Debonné White, from blended French hybrids.
Delaware, slightly sweet, soft.
Niagara, fruity, fragrant.
Vidal Blanc, dry varietal.

RED WINE

Debonné Red, full-bodied wine from hybrid grapes.

Debonné Rosé, semi-sweet, from hybrids.
River Rouge, blended concord, niagara, and hybrids.
Concord, a dry wine.
Pink Catawba, slightly sweet, aged in oak.

Price of wines: $2.70-$3.40.

Colonial Vineyards
ESTABLISHED 1977

6222 North State Route 48, Lebanon, OH 45036

Phone: 513-932-3842

Owner, Norman E. Greene.

Vineyards, 20 acres hybrids and catawba.

Fresh grapes or juices available in season for amateur winemakers.

Visiting: Daily 11:00 a.m.-8:00 p.m. Closed Sunday. Group wine tastings.

Storage capacity: 10,000 gallons.

Directions: Southwestern Ohio. Between Centerville and Lebanon on State Route 48. First farm south of village of Ridgeville.

Norman Greene's winemaking hobby looks less like a hobby and more like a full-time profession every day. However, Greene still travels frequently working full-time as a computer analyst, and still regards the big old tobacco barn winery and the fast developing vineyards as hobby and recreation. Perhaps that's because he has so many competent hands at home to help—wife Marion, son Michael, and daughter Jane. Daughter Norma thoughtfully provided an extra helper when she married David Young—they're on hand often. Daughter Suzanne, when we last checked, was about to marry and bring another part-time worker into the family. At a time when all tanks are full of must, and fast-ripening grapes must be picked and crushed, one might guess that

Norman and Marion Greene would heartily welcome another son-in-law!

The Greenes bought the "Riley Farm" (Rileys lived there for ninety years) in 1974, so their vineyards are well established; they are largely planted to French-American varieties of grapes.

Wines of Colonial Vineyards

WHITE WINE

Aurora, somewhat sweet.
Catawba, semi-sweet.
Niagara, semi-sweet.
Seyval Blanc, semi-sweet.
Villard Blanc, dry.

RED WINE

Baco Noir, dry.
De Chaunac, dry.
Foch, medium dry.

Price of wines: $3.60.

Dover Vineyards, Inc.
ESTABLISHED 1934

24945 Detroit Rd., Westlake, OH 44145

Phone: 216-871-0700

Owner, president and general manager: Zoltan Wolovitz.

Restaurant: Dover Chalet.

Home winemaking and beermaking supplies.

Vineyards: None.

Visiting: Winery is open to the public in the fall, or to groups by appointment.

Storage capacity: 180,000 gallons.

Directions: Westlake is west of Cleveland, 15 minutes from downtown.

Dover Chalet is a restaurant within a winery. It is attractive, comfortable, and offers its own wines to accompany lunch or dinner. All wines are made of native grapes in traditional styles, most mellow, and with varying degrees of sweetness.

The amateur winemaking supply business is also conducted here. Dover has anything you need along this line. "We've had an enormous wholesale and retail business in winemaking supplies for the last eight years," says Proprietor Wolovitz.

The restaurant specializes in seafood and Hungarian dishes. A typical dinner might cost $7.50.

Wines of Dover Vineyards

Dessert Wines, including port, sherry, muscatel (all 17 per cent alcohol).
Sparkling Wines, bulk or charmat process. Sparkling grape juice.
Scuppernong, from South Carolina grape of same name. Sherry-like flavor.

WHITE WINE

Cream Niagara
Dry Catawba
Rhine Wine, "extra dry."

RED WINE

Dry or *Sweet Concord*
Half and Half, half concord, half niagara.
Labrusca, mellow-medium-sweet.
Pink Catawba
Ohio Rosé

Price of wines: $1.95-about $4.08 (sparkling).

E. & K. Wine Company
ESTABLISHED 1863

220 East Water St., Sandusky, OH 44870

Phone: 419-627-9622

Officers: President, chairman, Edward L. Feick; general manager, winemaker, Clifford J. Gregory.

Vineyards: None. Grapes purchased locally for traditional Ohio wines.

Amateur winemaking supplies.

Visiting: Tuesday through Saturday 11:00 a.m.-5:00 p.m.; Summer, open at 10:00 a.m. Tours and tasting, $1.00 per person. No reservation needed in summer.

Storage capacity: 26,000 gallons.

Directions: On the downtown Sandusky waterfront (Lake Erie). By boat or car, easy to find.

This is a reactivated winery, in a landmark building, in a big winemaking center of yesteryear. The Engels and Krudwig Winery won awards for some of its bottles in the Paris Exposition of 1900. Present owners make wines from Ohio native grapes in the traditional way, and show visitors the ancient cellars.

Wines of E. & K. Wine Company

WHITE WINE

Catawba
Cream Catawba
Dry Catawba
Niagara

RED WINE

Concord
Sweet Concord
Mellow Monk Rosé

Red and White (concord and niagara).
Pink Catawba

Price of wines: $2.60.

Grand River Vineyard
ESTABLISHED 1971

5750 Madison Road, Madison, OH 44057

Phone: 216-298-9838 or 428-5054

President, Willett Worthy; vineyard manager, Mark Walker; cellar-master, Margaret Gerlosky.

Vineyards: 32 acres.

Visiting: Tours, tasting, Friday, Saturday, 1:00 p.m.-6:00 p.m. Open by reservation at other times and for private gatherings by reservation anytime.

Storage capacity: 25,000 gallons.

Directions: 3 miles south of Madison-Thompson exit of Interstate 90, on State 528.

Because crop limitation is necessary, if your goal is superior grapes for superior wines, Bill Worthy, ex-banker, is no longer able to supply good friend Tom Wykoff (Cedar Hill Wine Company) and other winemakers with vinifera and French hybrid grapes. He needs them all for his own chardonnay, seyval, vidal, and other wines. Before opening the family winery in 1978, Worthy had grapes and juice to spare, and a ready market for them.

One of the Midwest's most successful growers of vinifera, Worthy benefits from the influence of Lake Erie's waters in the northern Ohio climate. He has such success with chardonnay, sauvignon blanc, gamay beaujolais, and pinot noir that he doesn't mind the extra work of deep plowing to bury the vines in winter, and uncovering them in the spring. Gewürztraminer has been added to the vineyard to supplement vinifera vines already bearing.

Grand River Vineyard's most extensive plantings are of French hybrids, seyval blanc and chancellor, and the Worthys find a ready market for these two wines.

The winery is a rustic, L-shaped building situated in a wooded area next to the vineyard. One arm of the "L" is an open pavilion, where visitors can watch the crushing and pressing during harvest. The other arm houses a large party room with beamed ceiling, fireplace, and French doors opening into a large patio. The smaller tasting room, where the wines are sold, is equipped with an antique bar.

Carroll and Bill Worthy's daughter, Adrienne, has been such a great help in the family winery that her parents named one of the wines for her, a white blended wine that made its debut on Adrienne's twenty-first birthday. Adrienne's younger brother, John, enjoys working in the vineyard and being a source of summer jobs for his friends, his mother says. Carroll herself hardly sits around enjoying the busy scene. The painting and decorating, parties at the winery, day-to-day upkeep and sales of wine are her domain.

The Worthys say that the mainstay of their operation is Margaret Gerlosky, cellarmaster and vice-president of the company. The members of her husband's family are fruit growers and cidermakers in the Madison area. "Margaret has a real feel for winemaking from the vineyard to the selling process," says Carroll.

Wines of Grand River Vineyard

WHITE WINE

Chardonnay (vintage dated).
Vidal Blanc, semi-dry.
Vignoles, dry.
Seyval Blanc (best seller).

RED WINE

Chancellor, light, fruity.
Landot Noir, light, fruity.
Leon Millot, light, fruity.
Vinifera Rosé

Price of wines: $3.25-$8.50.

Hafle Vineyards
ESTABLISHED 1974

2369 Upper Valley Pike, Springfield, OH 45502

Phone: 513-399-2334 or 399-5742

Owner, Dan Hafle.

Vineyards: 39 acres hybrids and native grapes.

Visiting: Monday-Thursday 11:00 a.m.-8:00 p.m.; Friday, Saturday 11:00 a.m.-11:00 p.m.; Sunday noon-6:00 p.m. (carry-out only, no Sunday tasting). Other premises, 5010 South High St., Columbus, OH.

Storage capacity: 10,000 gallons.

Directions: ½ mile north of Upper Valley Mall on Upper Valley Pike, northwest of Springfield.

Dan and Lee Hafle (rhymes with safely) and sons Daniel and David have converted an ancient barn into a winery, but they cleverly kept the horse stalls and bull pen and turned them into tasting booths. Cheese and sausage snacks are available for the tastings.

The winery is in a rural setting, even though it is close to a large shopping mall. A hill obscures the look of civilization. The winery grounds are given over to bratwurst and wine parties with musical groups performing, several times each summer. The "brats" are cooked in Hafle wine. Sometimes there are corn roasts. In early September, the Upper Valley and Springfield Wine Festival takes place in the winery grounds.

Special programs are arranged for groups interested in learning about winemaking, after visiting hours are over.

The Columbus premises are a complete winery operation with thirty acres of vineyards at hand. The address, 5010 S. High Street, is also on U.S. 23 South, with which High Street merges south of the city.

The Hafles say there are good motels and excellent restaurants in their area, as well as "a terrific campground that offers fishing and swimming."

Wines of Hafle Vineyards

WHITE WINE

Ohio White, dry wine from villard blanc.
Ohio Sauterne, from blended hybrid grapes.

RED WINE

Ohio Red, dry wine from French hybrids chelois and baco.
De Chaunac, dry.
Concord, semi-sweet, some hybrid blending.
Vin Rosé, semi-dry.
Sangria, semi-sweet concord wine with citrus juices.

Price of wines: $2.75-$4.50.

Heineman Winery

ESTABLISHED 1897

Corner Catawba and Cherry Avenue, Put-in-Bay, OH 43456

Phone: 419-285-2811

President, H.F. Heineman; vice-president, secretary, L.V. Heineman; winemaker, Edward Heineman.

Vineyards: 35 acres native and hybrid grapes.

Visiting: 11:00 a.m.-5:00 p.m. May 25-Sept. 10. Tasting room 10:00 a.m.-10:00 p.m. Wine Garden. Special groups accommodated.

Storage capacity: 50,000 gallons.

Directions: By plane or boat from Sandusky.

Louis Heineman, third generation proprietor of this eighty-three-year-old Lake Erie Island winery, makes wines of traditional Ohio grapes, in the family's traditional style. In tune with the times, the Heinemans have recently added seyval, vidal, and de Chaunac to the roster. A wine garden built in 1977 has been expanded to accommodate thousands of summer visitors who come by plane and ferry boat. There were once other wineries on South Bass Island, but Heineman is the only one now, and is one of two left* (the other is Bretz) on what were once called Lake Erie's "wine islands."

Visitors to Heineman Winery may visit Crystal Cave which was discovered on the property in 1897. It is a small cave of large strontium crystals, located under the winery. A small fee is charged for the tour and visit to Crystal Cave, which is well worth seeing.

Wines of Heineman Winery
(all bear the Heineman's Lake Erie Islands label)

WHITE WINE

Delaware
Dry Catawba
Seyval Blanc
Sauterne
Vidal Blanc

RED WINE

Burgundy
Claret
Sweet Concord
Sweet Belle (catawba and concord).
Pink Catawba
Rosé

Price of wines: About $2.75–$3.90.

Heritage Vineyards
ESTABLISHED 1978

6020 Wheelock Road, West Milton, OH 45383.

Phone: 513-698-5369

---

* Meier's Isle St. George, on maps as North Bass Island, is covered with vineyards, but there's no winery.

Owners, Edward W. Stefanko, Wallace J. Zins, John F. Feltz.

Vineyards: 20 acres.

Visiting: Wednesday through Saturday 1:00-9:00 p.m. Tours on request, wine tastings by appointment.

Storage capacity: 15,000 gallons.

Directions: West of Interstate 75 (Dayton Airport vicinity) on SR 571 to Wheelock Road. One mile south.

Three families ("We have lots of children to help with the picking") are associated in this handsome new winery located in a 100-year-old barn. It has been remodeled to feature a cedarwood "chalet" tasting room with a second story open loft where visitors may enjoy the wines while looking out upon vineyards and meadows. Bread and cheese trays are available for those who wish to snack while sipping Heritage Red or Seyval Blanc.

Most Heritage Vineyards wines are made from French-American hybrid grapes; the vineyards were planted, beginning in 1972, with 12,000 vines, most of which are now bearing. There is even a Heritage Vineyards Ohio champagne, made by the *méthode champenoise*.

The owners hope to double production. They were delighted with their successful first year (1979) and a production of 10,000 gallons of wine.

Wines of Heritage Vineyards

Champagne made of hybrid grape varieties.

WHITE WINE

Aurora, semi-sweet.
Heritage Vin Blanc, dry.
Niagara, sweet.
Seyval Blanc, semi-sweet.
Seyve-Villard 12375, semi-dry.

RED WINE

Baco Noir, dry.
Chelois, semi-dry.
De Chaunac, dry.

Heritage Rouge, semi-dry blend of native, hybrid grapes.
Heritage Red, semi-sweet blend.
Maréchal Foch, semi-dry.
Red Catawba, semi-sweet.
Light Red Concord, sweet.
Heritage Rosé, semi-dry blend.

Price of wines: $2.50-$3.25.

Klingshirn Winery
ESTABLISHED 1935

33050 Weber Road, Avon Lake, OH 44012

Phone: 216-933-6666

Owner, Allan A. Klingshirn; bookkeeper, Barbara Klingshirn.

Vineyards: 10 acres native grapes.

Visiting: Weekdays 12:00 p.m.-6:00 p.m.; Saturdays 9:00 a.m.-6:00 p.m. Closed Sunday. In season, fresh grape juices available for amateur winemakers.

Storage capacity: 30,000 gallons.

Directions: Off Route 83 between Routes 6 and 2, west side of Route 83.

During Prohibition, there was a large market for grapes—not surprisingly—and Ohio farmers in the Lake Erie region grew many varieties. When drinking was legal again, growers around Avon Lake didn't know what to do with their surplus fruit. So they formed a cooperative and began making wine—that is, Albert Klingshirn began making wine in his basement for them. Before he knew it, and without his really wanting it to happen, Albert Klingshirn's home became the Klingshirn winery. That was in 1935.

Today his son Allan and wife Barbara, with the help of their four children and sundry cousins, operate an expanded winery. Says Barbara happily, "At last, I think we've got it packaged!" They had planned to expand in 1977 with a tasting room addition, but that year they lost eighty percent of their crop, and expansion was out. In 1979, they managed it, and best of all, could move the press from another farm to the winery.

Of the four young Klingshirns, Ann, Jim, Neil, and Lee, the youngest, Lee, is the one who wants to study enology and viticulture. His mother says that he's very good at trimming vines.

The Klingshirns grow only native grapes and have no ambitions to become larger. They sell lots of concord, catawba, and niagara juices to "do-it-yourselfers," but give notice that home winemakers must come for it immediately after the crush, as they have no facilities for keeping fresh grape juice.

Wines of Klingshirn

Cherry Wine

WHITE WINE

Sauterne, dry.
Catawba, dry.
Haut Sauterne, semi-sweet.
Niagara, semi-sweet.
Niagara, dry.

RED WINE

Concord, dry.
Concord, sweet.
Pink Catawba
Vin Rosé

Price of wines: About $2.25.

Le Boudin Vineyard and Winery

ESTABLISHED 1968

R.R. 3, Box 172, Cardington, OH 43315

Phone: 419-768-2091

Owner-winemaker, Mrs. Ruth W. Hubbell; vineyard manager and winemaker, I. Carroll Hubbell.

Vineyard: 6 acres hybrids.

Visiting: noon-midnight; live country music on weekends.

Home winemaking supplies.

Storage capacity: 15,000 gallons.

Directions: On County Road 25, 5 miles east of Fulton and State Highway 61, and east of I-71 from Cleveland to Columbus.

Le Boudin Winery happened all of a sudden. When Ruth Le Boudin Hubbell's first husband was living, the couple raised longhorn cattle. Le Boudin helped install a water system for a winery in southern Ohio and when he returned home he said to Ruth, "Guess what we're going to do! We're going to start our own winery!" Within a week, Ruth Hubbell says, the longhorns were gone and the winery was on the way.

French hybrid vines were then planted. Some of the winery equipment came from the old Strait winery in Columbus, which lost out to an airport, and the Strait label is retained for several wines still enjoyed by a sizable number of Ohioans. The concords are bought from other growers since the Hubbells grow only French hybrids. Philip Wagner gave invaluable help to the budding winery, Ruth Hubbell told us.

Le Boudin died in 1972, and Ruth Le Boudin later married a kindred soul, Carroll Hubbell, who manages the vineyard. Together they make the wines of Le Boudin.

A feature of the winery is a long bar that will accommodate from fifty to 100 wine-sippers. Amish cheese and cheese pizzas are available. New Year's Eve celebrations at the winery are something special and so is the Labor Day pig roast.

The wines are distributed in Columbus as well as sold at the winery.

Wines of Le Boudin Winery

WHITE WINE

American Sauterne
Apple Wine
Niagara, dry.
White Wine, French hybrid blend.

RED WINE

Ohio Concord (Strait's label), 2 wines, one 16% alcohol.
Niagara Concord
Red Wine, French hybrid blend.
Rosé Wine
Pink Catawba

Price of wines: About $2.75.

Lukens Vineyard
ESTABLISHED 1978

10104 SR 73 E, Harveysburg, OH 45032

Phone: 513-897-1776

Owners: Chairman, Donald E. Lukens; president, Allen Osborn.

Vineyard: 20 acres.

Visiting: Monday through Saturday, noon-9:00 p.m.

Storage capacity: 3,500 gallons.

Directions: On state Route 73, three miles west of junction with Interstate 71.

The newest in a cluster of small wineries in the Cincinnati area, Lukens Vineyard, is situated on farmland owned by the Lukens family for more than 100 years. The winery tasting room was converted from an old machine shed. The location is very close to Caesar's Creek Lake, a resort area that draws half a million visitors every year. "Buz" Lukens and Allen Osborn don't need to advertise for customers.

The two men enjoy wine and are enthusiastic about playing a part in restoring vineyards to southwestern Ohio and a wine drinking tradition to their state. Lukens is a state senator whose political activities have brought him national recognition. He served seven years in the U.S. Air Force, speaks several foreign languages fluently, and has carried out assignments for the U.S. government in other lands. He has been a U.S. congressman.

Both the Osborn and Lukens families live in Middletown. For Allen Osborn, a former accountant, the winery has become a full-time career.

Grapes planted include de Chaunac, seyval blanc, catawba and concord. At this time seventy-five percent of the winery's grapes are purchased from other growers.

Wines of Lukens Vineyard

WHITE WINE

Blanc du Lac, dry blend.
Niagara, semi-sweet.

RED WINE

Rouge du Lac, dry.
Catawba Rosé, sweet.
Concord Rosé, sweet.

Price of wines: $3.00-$3.25.

McIntosh's Ohio Valley Wines
ESTABLISHED 1972

R.R. 1 Bethel, OH 45106

Phone: 513-379-1159 (Residence)

Owners, Charles and Alice McIntosh.

Vineyard: 17½ acres native and hybrid grapes.

Visiting: All year 1:00 p.m.-midnight. Closed Sunday and Monday. Pizzas or cheese tray available with wine.

Storage capacity: 22,000 gallons.

Directions: From Cincinnati Highway 125 east through Bethel; take 2nd road to left, Spring Grove Road, to winery. (Spring Grove changes name at Brown County line becoming Bethel and New Hope Road). From Columbus Highway 71 to Wilmington, Highway 68 south, turn right into Bethel and New Hope Road, to winery.

Community service is one of the functions of many small wineries, but I know of none more actively engaged in community projects than the Charles McIntoshes. In late summer, the winery is a Bike-a-thon stop for youngsters raising funds for the American Cancer Society. Soft drinks are served, and several women's groups provide food for the young people. Girl Scouts, Boy Scouts and the Brown County Historical Society also gather here. On Saturdays there are afternoon wagon tours through the vineyards at 1:30 p.m. and 5:30 p.m.

Grapes are harvested by young people from a school for the mentally retarded. In age, they range from eighteen to twenty-eight. They do an excellent job, McIntosh says. The winery is actually a small restaurant, as the McIntoshes make pizza and offer good cheese from Chalet Cheese Cooperative, Monroe, Wisconsin. There are tables with candlelight inside the winery, a patio with picnic tables outside.

One senses that the McIntoshes thoroughly enjoy all this happy activity, but how Farmer McIntosh finds time for it is a wonder. On the 350 acre farm, in addition to vineyards, he grows sixty acres of grain, 225 acres of soybeans, and twelve acres of strawberries. They make a little strawberry wine for themselves, McIntosh says.

He grew up on the farm and yearned to get back into farming during the years when he owned a trucking business. When he thought *farm*, he also began thinking *winery*. He began reading books including Philip Wagner's *A Wine Grower's Guide*, and later, McIntosh obtained some of his winery equipment from Wagner, including the crusher-stemmer and filtering equipment.

Hybrid grapes grown in the McIntosh vineyards include seyval blanc, aurora, de Chaunac, and baco noir. The favorite wine of visitors is the sweet rosé made by combining the native concord with the French hybrid aurora.

For hospitality and charm, McIntosh's Ohio Valley Winery is hard to match.

Wines of McIntosh's Ohio Valley Winery

WHITE WINE

Catawba, dry.
Catawba, sweet.
Niagara, semi-sweet.
Sauterne, seyval blanc grapes.

RED WINE

Pink Catawba
Rosé (aurora and concord), sweet.
Concord, semi-sweet.
Red Wine, dry, from hybrid grapes.

Price of wines: $2.75-$3.25.

Mantey Vineyards, Inc.
ESTABLISHED 1880

917 Bardshar Road, Sandusky, OH 44870

Phone: 419-625-5474

President and sales manager, Norman E. Mantey; winemaker, Jack Cupp, Jr.; vineyard manager, Donald Mantey.

Vineyards: 40 acres native, hybrid, and vinifera grapes. Also grapes from 200 acres leased.

Home winemaking supplies.

Salesroom hours: Daily 9:00 a.m.-5:00 p.m. Saturdays 9:00 a.m.-noon.

Storage capacity: 100,000 gallons.

Directions: Far southwest corner of Sandusky. Intersection U.S. 6 and Rt. 2 (that's ½ block off U.S. 2 bypass around Sandusky).

"We've never closed since my grandfather founded the winery back in 1880," says Paul Mantey, one of four third-generation Manteys, who has now retired. "We made it through Prohibition just selling grape juice." The other Manteys are Norman, Donald, and their sister Marie Herman, who runs the office.

As winemaker, Paul Mantey was first to make a pink catawba, but, he says, he was a little ahead of the times on that one, and big Eastern wineries later capitalized on his idea.

Baco noir and seyval blanc are the first hybrid grape wines from

Mantey Vineyards, but there are likely to be more. "Blue Face" is a concord wine named for what it was called in earlier days. Customers would ask for "a gallon of 'blue face.' "

The Baco receives royal treatment as a fine wine—two years in oak, followed by six months or more of bottle-aging.

Mantey is one of the largest producers in Ohio with a capacity of 100,000 gallons. The family employs ten people in the vineyards and winery, and at harvest time, they take on about twenty-five more.

Mantey is a 20-minute drive from Mon Ami.

Wines of Mantey Vineyards

Cream Sherry, *White Port* (a specialty).

WHITE WINE

Cream Catawba, light and mellow.
Ohio Catawba, dry, crisp.
Seyval Blanc, dry wine from French hybrid grapes.

RED WINE

Baco Noir, robust, aged in oak at least two years.
Pink Catawba
Vin Rosé, medium sweet party wine, blend of native and hybrid grapes.
Mellow Concord, medium sweet.
Concord, a dry dinner wine.
Blue Face, medium-dry concord.
Burgundy, a blend of labrusca and hybrid grapes, dry.

Price of wines: About $2.00.

Note: Meier's Wine Cellars bought Mantey and Mon Ami in mid-1980.

Markko Vineyard
ESTABLISHED 1968

R.D. 2, South Ridge Road, Conneaut, OH 44030

Phone: 216-593-3197

Partner and winemaker, Arnulf Esterer.

Vineyard: 10 acres vinifera chardonnay and white riesling; cabernet sauvignon.

Visiting: Monday-Saturday 11:00 a.m.-6:00 p.m. Tastings by appointment.

Storage capacity: 5,000 gallons.

Directions: Kingsville exit from I-90 between Cleveland and Erie, Pa. North on South Ridge Road.

Markko is a little winery (in the woods) which produces three wines from vinifera grapes: white riesling, chardonnay, and cabernet sauvignon. Arnulf (Arnie) Esterer is satisfied with nothing but top quality, and he is willing to work hard.

Fortune smiled on the Esterers (Kate and the four children all help) when they chose the woodland site for their winery. It is only three miles from Lake Erie Shores, and winters are kinder there than to vineyards a few miles farther inland. Lake Erie's summer-warmed waters take the bitterness out of winter cold. That's one reason why the Esterers can grow classical vinifera grapes.

The other reason is summed up in the word "dedication." Arnie Esterer's interest in grapes and wine grew naturally from an existing appreciation for wine and its healthful properties as a food beverage. He went to see Dr. Konstantin Frank, the pioneer vinifera grower of New York, and then began to study the feasibility of growing classical grapes in Ohio. At the time, Esterer was a manager at the Union Carbide Metal Company and lived in Ashtabula, so the Esterers chose a nearby site. Not only does it benefit from the watery environment, but the soil is silt-loam, very good footing for vines.

Dr. Frank has watched the growing vineyard with interest. The vines are from his nursery stock, but Frank refused to sell Esterer more than 500 vines at a time, until he could see how well they were doing. He now thoroughly approves, and Esterer says he is grateful for Dr. Frank's support and assistance through the years.

Ashtabula stockbroker, Thomas H. Hubbard, is Esterer's partner, and all "which way to go now" decisions are made jointly. Both men are proud of the ardent reception given the wines since the first vintage in 1972. In blind tastings, which included both California and German rieslings, Markko's Johannisberg Riesling has been taken for the "original" German wine, with top ranking. The riesling has the typical flowery nose and the chardonnay is pleasantly oaky and spicy from being aged in small French oak barrels, after fermentation in stainless steel. Markko Vineyard's 1979 Johannisberg Riesling Reserve tied for "Best of Show" award in Wineries Unlimited 1980 Eastern Wine Competition. The other top wine was Golden Rain Tree (Indiana) Criterion White wine.

Note: If you have dinner at the King's Tavern, Kingsville, you'll be able to complement your meal with a Markko Vineyard wine of a recent vintage from the restaurant's showy winecellar.

Wines of Markko Vineyard

WHITE WINE

Chardonnay, estate-bottled, vintage-dated.
Riesling, estate-bottled, vintage, in several styles.
Underridge, blend of riesling, chardonnay.

RED WINE

Cabernet Sauvignon
Chambourcin
Markko Red, hybrid blend with some cabernet.

Price of wines: Most $4.98-$6.98.

Marlo Winery
ESTABLISHED 1978

Rt. 1, 3636 State Rt. 47, Fort Laramie, OH 45845

Phone: 513-295-3232

Owners, Milo and Margaret Strozensky.

Vineyards: 3.5 acres native and hybrid vines.

Storage capacity: 3,000 gallons.

Visiting: Wednesday, Thursday, 5:00 p.m.-9:00 p.m.; Friday, 5:00 p.m.-10:00 p.m.; Saturday, 2:00 p.m.-10:00 p.m.

Gift shop, "The Purple Thumb," wine related and other gifts. Snacks available at the winery Tasting Room.

Directions: 10 miles west of Interstate 75, or ¼ mile east of Highway 66, on Highway 47.

Marlo is a three-generation family winery. Milo's parents are active workers as are the Strozensky children, Mark and Michelle, when they are not in school. All hands are needed—"From the vineyard to the bottle, the family handles the entire operation, including the tasting room and gift shop," says Milo. That's no small accomplishment, considering that Margaret works full time as an executive secretary at the local hospital and her husband has not one, but two other occupations. He is a sales engineer by profession, and also serves as pastor to a local congregation.

The Strozensky family caters to private parties and club meetings at the winery, and offers on Saturdays a $1.50 "mini potpourri" of cheese, crackers, beef stick, vegetables and dip to enjoy with wine. Snacks are always available with wine tastings.

Wines of Marlo Winery

WHITE WINE

Niagara, semi-sweet.
Seyval Blanc, dry.

RED WINE

Concord, sweet.
Pink Concord, semi-sweet.
Pink Catawba, sweet.
Foch, dry.

Price of wines: $3.00.

Meier's Wine Cellars, Inc.
ESTABLISHED 1895

6955 Plainfield Pike, Silverton, Cincinnati, OH 45236

Phone: 513-891-2900

Owners: Paramount Distillers; president, Robert C. Gottesman; vice-president-secretary, Gerald R. Vitek; vineyard manager, Dale Burris; senior enologist, Donald Bower; winemaker, Meredith Lewis.

Vineyards: 350 acres, Isle St. George. Grapes also purchased from New York, Pennsylvania, Missouri, Canada.

Visiting and winery tours: 10:00 a.m.-3:00 p.m., tours on the hour. Call to reserve for a large group.

Storage capacity: 2,500,000 gallons.

Restaurant at the winery: Open Monday-Saturday 11:30 a.m.-2:30 p.m. Dinners Friday and Saturday 6:00 p.m.-1:00 a.m.

Directions: From downtown Cincinnati, 10 miles. Take I-71 north to Exit 12, Montgomery Road; left on Montgomery Road 3 traffic lights to Plainfield Pike; right turn on Plainfield, 1,000 feet to the winery.

In the lifetime of Henry O. Sonneman, a beloved and respected figure in the American wine industry, Meier's was the oldest and biggest winery in Ohio, and a family company. In 1928, Sonneman had bought Meier's Grape Juice Company, and after the repeal of Prohibition five years later, he set about restoring Ohio's reputation as a wine-producing state. He traveled to vineyards all over the world looking for new ideas and dreaming of re-establishing grape culture along the Ohio River, where Nicholas Longworth had produced his "divine" catawba more than a century earlier.

Paramount Distillers took over Meier's subsequent to Sonneman's death in 1974 and sold Sonneman's 100 acres of Ohio River vineyard land,* finding it more practical to concentrate on the 350 acres of catawba, French-American hybrid grapes, and some chardonnay and

---

* Half of the vineyards were leased by the purchasers to Kenneth Schuchter and John Emmering for growing hybrid varieties to supply Valley Vineyards and other wineries.

riesling growing on Isle St. George, in Lake Erie. Catawba grapes had been growing there since the early 1800s. Sonneman planted the others. To add to the extensive property on Isle St. George, Paramount has recently bought the 139-acre Lonz estate on Middle Bass Island,* complete with its rather bizarre chateau. The land had been out of production for ten years, but the property had once been a lure for tourists, and perhaps can be again.

Meier's has a new line of island wines, and now produces both chardonnay and white riesling. But the company has kept such old favorite wines as the famous rich, sweet cream sherry known as No. 44. Now as before, Meier's sherries are aged for years in barrels in the out-of-doors.

In keeping with changing American tastes, some of the table wines are being made lighter and fruitier. Don Bower has also produced a wine called Fu Lu, to meet the need for a wine suited to Chinese food.

Nothing is static at Paramount's Meier's. Visitors can see the entire winemaking process. The restaurant is attractive and provides excellent food, and the landscaped gardens offer al fresco cheese and wine in summer. The best and favorite old wines are available, as well as many new ones.

Wines of Meier's Wine Cellars

Sherries, ports, sparkling wines, apple, blackberry, spice wine, cider, non-alcoholic grape juices, generic wines, others.

WHITE WINE

Catawba
Island White
La Brusca Bianco
Chardonnay
Johannisberg Riesling

RED WINE

Baco Noir
Chelois
Catawba Rosé
Island Red

* We have learned that Meier's purchased two other small Ohio wineries, as well. They are Mantey's and Mon Ami.

Island Rosé
La Brusca Rubio
La Brusca Rosato

Price of Wines: $2.00-$7.00.

Moyer Vineyards
ESTABLISHED 1973

U.S. Highway 52, Manchester, OH 45144

Phone: 513-549-2957

Owner, Kenneth L. Moyer.

Vineyards: 12 acres.

Visiting: Monday-Thursday, 11:30 a.m.-9:00 p.m.; Friday, Saturday, open till 10:00 p.m. Closed Sunday.

Restaurant hours: 11:30 a.m.-10:00 p.m. daily except Sunday.

Storage capacity: 10,000 gallons.

Directions: 4 miles west of Manchester, approximately 70 miles east of Cincinnati, on U.S. 52.

Ken and Mary Moyer were living in Mexico City where Moyer was consultant for a ceramics tile plant when word came that the couple were being transferred to Morocco. "That did it!" said Mary.

The ceramics engineer, who had managed several plants in Ohio prior to the Mexican assignment, and who had grown grapes for years to make wine for the family, decided there were better things in life than running tile factories. Why not open a winery?

The Moyers didn't return to Ohio and its fruitful river valley without looking around first. They traipsed through seven states hunting for the right vineyard site.

"We found our spot in 1972," Mary Moyer said. "There were sixty-five acres of land, including a half-mile stretch along the Ohio River. It had been a truck stop." What a beautiful truck stop was then sacrificed to grapes and a winery! And ultimately to a restaurant which "just happened," but lures people seventy miles "up" from Cincinnati and fifty miles "down" from Portsmouth. Guests come in their boats in the summertime and dock them on the riverbank while they eat.

The Moyer wines are made from French hybrid grapes, sixty percent of them from their own vineyards, the rest from other growers.

The restaurant that "just happened" was born out of "a few cheeses and some soup"—something to go with wine. Now *tournedos, boeuf bourguignon*, poached scallops in white wine, veal Orloff, and other entrees may be ordered. Of course, there's a salad bar, and desserts include such delicacies as French chocolate almond pie and raw apple walnut cake.

The wine list at Moyer Restaurant is short. Just seven choices, but you can buy by the glass as well as the bottle. No beer or soft drinks are served. The highest-priced entree is crab supreme at $9.25.

Wines of Moyer Vineyards

Champagne Brut

WHITE WINE

Moyer White Wine, crisp, dry.
River Valley White, moderately sweet.

RED WINE

Moyer Red Wine, robust, dry.
River Valley Red, mellow, moderately sweet.
Moyer Rosé, dry and crisp.
River Valley Rosé, sweeter.

Price of wines: Around $3.85; Sparkling wine $6.20. By the glass $1.00-$2.50.

Steuk Wine Company

ESTABLISHED 1855

1001 Fremont Ave., Sandusky, OH 44870

Phone: 419-625-0803

Owner, William C. Steuk; general manager, Tim Parker.

Vineyards: 4½ acres traditional Ohio grapes.

Visiting: Daily 8:00 a.m.-6:00 p.m.

Storage capacity: 10,000 gallons.

Directions: Located in the Sandusky-Fremont interchange (Route 6 exit) of Route 2 bypass.

William C. Steuk is the fifth generation owner of the Steuk Winery, one of the oldest in the country, and one of the rare few which have remained in one family.

Tim Parker, like Steuk, comes from a long line of Sandusky citizens, most of them medical men—father, uncle, grandfather. "My grandfather was a horse-and-buggy doctor," says Tim, whose scientific leanings led him into pre-med studies. Then came a year in Germany, a degree in science from the University of Toledo, and pursuit of a master's degree in chemistry. From high school days, he had worked off and on in the Steuk winery, and while engaged in writing his thesis found that what he really wanted to do was make wine, not finish his master's studies.

William Steuk, senior, had died, and the present owner of the small but ancient cellar and vineyard wasn't ready to take over. He is a successful, full-time practicing attorney.

The wines Parker makes are the same traditional wines of Ohio, and they are sold only at the winery. Where else can you buy a bottle of Black Pearl, made from a grape developed by a man named Kaspar Schraidt of Put-in-Bay?

Wines of Steuk

Sparkling Wines, including pink, brut, extra dry, Sparkling Burgundy, Sparkling Catawba.

Traditional Native Grape Wines including among white wines: Missouri Riesling, Dry Delaware, Sweet Niagara, Sweet and Dry Catawba. Red Wines: Sweet and Dry Concord.
Unusual Varietal Wines include Beta, Black Pearl, Clinton, Elvira, Montefiore.

Price of wines: $2.85-$5.85; sparkling wines $6.40-$6.75.

Stone Quarry Vineyards
ESTABLISHED 1979

Waterford, OH 45786

Phone: 614-984-4423

Owners, Thomas and Timothy Simpson.

Vineyards: 28 acres leased; 8 acres producing.

Amateur wine supplies.

Visiting: April to late October 10:00 a.m.-8:00 p.m.; winter hours 10:00 a.m.-6:00 p.m. Usually open Sundays, but no Sunday sales permitted.

Storage capacity: 1,000 gallons (space for 12,000 gallons).

Directions: From Columbus east on I-70 to Zanesville; State 60 south to Beverly. Rt. 339 across bridge to Waterford.

Stone Quarry Vineyards is a father and son operation. Father Tom Simpson and son Tim were both working in various capacities at the Fawcett Center for Tomorrow, a continuing education facility of the University of Ohio, Columbus. In the spring of 1977, during a seminar of the Ohio Wine Producers Association, they learned of a neglected vineyard that needed managing.

"I guess you could say I was an amateur winemaker who just got carried away," says Tom. "We took over and started planning."

The Simpsons opened their winery in the late fall of 1979. The building they occupy had been a wool warehouse before the turn of the century. There is plenty of room for expansion in the 32′ × 80′ two-story structure; initially, the space required was only one corner.

The Simpsons took a lesson from the Gallo brothers in California, making contracts with three growers to grow the grapes they need and agreeing to take all of the production. This plan works to the satisfaction of both grower and producer, Tom Simpson believes. He spends full time on the winery, while Tim, in his early twenties, works for a printing company to keep the fledgling enterprise funded.

In the spring of 1980 an ox roast, spaghetti dinner, tractor pull, and street dance established the new winery in the communities of Beverly and Waterford, situated on opposite sides of the Muskingum River, which empties into the Ohio a few miles south at Marietta. The two-day May fest is expected to be an annual event. Although Waterford township is "dry," the local ordinance applies not to the winery but only to retail stores; however, no Sunday sales are permitted. Retail outlets for Stone Quarry wines are located in Cambridge and Columbus.

Simpson senior told us that the devastating winters of 1976 and 1977 had pretty much determined what grape varieties would do well in the vineyards they supervise. Many white grape varieties were killed, but aurora and vidal survived, "and we have delaware coming on." As for red wine varieties of grapes, "Maréchal Foch came on like gang-busters!"

Four wines were introduced at the winery's opening.

Wines of Stone Quarry Vineyards

WHITE WINE

Dry White (Aurora and vidal blend).

RED WINE

Dry Red (predominantly Foch).
Pink Catawba, sweet.
Pioneer Red, sweet.

Price of wines: $2.75.

Warren J. Sublette Winery Company

(The Fountain Wine Stube)
ESTABLISHED 1975

2260 Central Parkway West, Cincinnati, OH 45214

Phone: 513-861-3248

President-winemaker, Warren J. Sublette; cellarmaster, Lou Lynch; sales manager, Steve Boston; office manager, Sam Williams.

Vineyards: None, grapes purchased.

Visiting: Monday-Saturday 11:00 a.m.-6:00 p.m. (Live music Friday, Saturday). Tours other times by appointment.
Restaurant*
Storage capacity: 20,000 gallons.

Directions: Northbound or southbound on I-75, Hopple Street Exit across interstate to Central Parkway. Right to winery 1 mile, on left. From downtown Cincinnati: Central Parkway about 1 mile north of Music Hall, on right.

This huge old stone building, constructed in 1850 and built into a hill-side, was a brewery for most of its life. Tales are told about what went on there during Prohibition, when the brewery became an illegal distillery that helped supply the Midwest with firewater. Its first floor was coated with sheet metal so that the approach of federal agents was noisy enough to sound a warning. At the first metallic clanking, it is said, the distillery equipment was rolled on wheels through a concealed tunnel into the next building, and with it disappeared the distilling crew. The "revenooers" found no trace of any forbidden activity, but they may have had their suspicions.

All the fun and games are legal now—the wine, the cafe atmosphere, the band that plays for your enjoyment. The Fountain Wine Stube is a happy place, whether you're there to drink Foch Nouveau wine and munch cheese, or have come with a group that has scheduled a full course dinner*, with a wine-tasting and lecture first. The big party room can accommodate 200 guests.

* At press time the restaurant was closed. Sublette was unsure whether it would re-open.

Sublette is a former industrial engineer. He enjoys serving and selling the wines he makes from French hybrid grapes. He's had plenty of winemaking experience, for he began this phase of his career as assistant manager for Wistar Marting's Tarula Farms Winery, and later was winemaker for Fountain Wine Cellars before taking over that enterprise.

Grapes come in for crushing on the top level of the winery, since it is cut into the hill. Fermenting equipment and wine barrels for aging and storing the wines are also on this level. The music, wine drinking, and at times, fine dining take place below.

Wines of Warren J. Sublette

WHITE WINE

Aurora, dry.
Blanc de Noirs, dry, fruity.
Vidal Blanc, vintage.
Seyval Blanc
Villard Blanc
Riverboat White, semi-sweet.

RED WINE

Baco Noir, dry, robust varietal.
Baco Rosé, dry blend of vintages.
Chancellor
Chelois Noir, "dry and mellow".
Maréchal Foch
Foch Nouveau, young, dry, fruity.
Catawba Rosé

Price of wines: $2.40-$3.95.

Tarula Winery
ESTABLISHED 1965

1786 Creek Road, Clarksville, OH 45113

Phone: 513-289-2181

Owner, Gregory Hayward.

Vineyards: 4½ acres; 60 percent grapes purchased.

Visiting: Winery closed January-mid-March, some visiting by appointment. Mid-March-June, 5:00 p.m.-9:00 p.m.; Saturday noon-9:00 p.m.; June-August, noon-9:00 p.m.; September-January, 5:00 p.m.-9:00 p.m.; Saturday noon-9:00 p.m. Closed Sundays.

Antiques, cheese for sale at winery. Parties, receptions, fishing and wine tastings can be arranged.

Storage capacity: 5,000 gallons.

Directions: One mile out of Clarksville on Creek Road. Or directly off State 22 and 23 between state routes 350 and 380. Cincinnati area.

"We don't know whether we found Tarula, or Tarula found us," Chris Hayward exults. "We feel that we were meant to be here. It's heaven, and home!"

The feeling is understandable when you learn that Chris and Greg, both school teachers, had planned to buy another farm and grow wine grapes, but the deal fell through after they'd sold their Cincinnati house. By a stroke of luck, the homeless young family (there are two small children) persuaded the management of Tarula Farms to sell the winery. It had been closed for more than a year after the death of Wistar Marting, the proprietor, who had been a pioneer in Ohio's small winery revival. The deal was made in three feet of snow after the 1978 blizzard, and the winery was opened in March of '79.

The Haywards have been very busy since then, re-establishing the winery and restoring the farm house, which was built in 1817. They don't plan to rush either project. They run the farm and winery as well as Chris's antique business (everything hangs on the walls of the tasting room) while holding down full-time teaching schedules, so they admit to "screwy" visiting hours. Tours and tastings can be arranged, however.

Greg, who teaches social studies, is a graduate of the University of Michigan and holds a master's degree from Xavier University. Chris is an art teacher. Both have a background in home winemaking and Greg is well-known as a helpful advisor to amateurs with problems.

With the farm the Haywards acquired a large fish pond filled with fish swimming around waiting to be caught and skilleted. They can sit, in the rare leisure moments, on the barn patio and look out over vineyards and a beautiful valley where deer and other wildlife abound. They believe they've stumbled into an Ohio paradise.

Wines of Tarula Winery

WHITE WINE

Tarula White (Seyval blanc), dry.
Country White, native grapes, sweet.

RED WINE

Tarula Red (de Chaunac), dry.
Country Red (concord), sweet.
Country Rosé (concord), sweet.

Price of wines: $2.50-$3.50.

Valley Vineyards Farm, Inc.

ESTABLISHED 1969

2041 E. U.S. 22-3, Morrow, OH 45152

Phone: 513-899-2485

President, Kenneth Schuchter; vice-president, Jim Schuchter; general manager and winemaker, James McCann.

Vineyards: 45 acres.

Winemaking supplies, fresh juices in season. Programs for clubs, receptions catered.

Visiting: Monday-Thursday 11:00 a.m.-8:00 p.m. Friday, Saturday 11:00 a.m.-11:00 p.m. Closed Sunday.

Storage capacity: 75,000 gallons.

Directions: From Cincinnati: I-71 or 75 to I-275. (Circle Freeway) east. East on 275 to U.S. 22 and State Rt. 3 Exit 50, Montgomery Road. Right on routes 22 and 3 for 11½ miles.

Before a certain significant evening, which changed their lives, neither Ken nor Marge Schuchter had ever had a glass of wine other than "a little Mogen David in the glass of 7-Up" at family gatherings on Christmas.

Then Marge, now secretary at the local high school, made a political speech at Wilmington, and the couple were invited to dinner afterward by Tony Williams, president of the Young Republicans of Wilmington.

As Marge tells the story, "Ken and Tony hit it off from the beginning. Both enjoyed farming, Ken, our truck farm and Tony, his 2,000 acres of corn, and hog raising. That evening, five couples consumed ten bottles of Lancers wine, and we all loved the wine and the relaxation produced by it. Tony said to Ken, 'Why don't you grow some grapes and make some of this stuff?' Ken said, 'Let's do it!' "

Later discussions raised the level of enthusiasm. Ken attended a meeting in Batavia, Ohio sponsored by Ohio State, and presided over by Dr. Garth Cahoon, well-known authority on grape-growing. The purpose was to encourage farmers to plant small acreages of grapes in a revival of winegrowing in the area.

His excitement high, Ken Schuchter ordered 12,500 vines of the kinds recommended, thinking to plant two acres of available land.

Continues Marge: "He went to another meeting, and Dr. Cahoon asked him what was his interest. Ken said he was getting into the grape business like these other farmers and had ordered 12,500 vines. With that, everyone in the room turned to look at Ken. It was an embarrassing moment when Ken was told that his vines would plant twenty acres and make him the second largest grower in the state!" The nursery from which the vines had been ordered told Schuchter they hadn't sold that many vines in forty-five years of operation. But they refused to take any of them back.

Pride prevailed, and the two acres grew into twenty. Then came another rude shock. Ken Schuchter learned that grape vines do not produce fruit for several years!

That both Ken and Marge can relate this hilarious story with great enjoyment tells you something about the attractive couple, who now are among the leaders of Midwestern winegrowing.

Ken, Marge, Ken's partner, his brother Jim, and Jim's wife Pat are proprietors of one of the most handsome wineries in Ohio. It was built into a huge old barn, and there's room for all kinds of tastings and buffet dinners for small or large groups. Spacious grounds surround the winery, where the annual Ohio Wine Festival takes place in September.

Something is always going on at Valley Vineyards Farm.

The Schuchters grow twenty-three varieties of grapes including native, hybrid, and vinifera varieties. The two acres of vinifera planted in 1974 include riesling, chardonnay, pinot noir, and merlot. Of the eleven wines they now have available, one varietal, Blue Eye, is unique. No other winery to my knowledge makes wine from Blue Eye grapes.

All the Schuchters are much involved in the winery, including son and daughter, Angela and Kenny.

The women who prune and pick grapes are the girls who went to school with Ken, and there are now six women who are competent helpers in the hospitality room. Valley Vineyards is growing.

And what of Tony Williams, who got the Schuchters into this, and who for a time was a partner?

"He remains a best friend, customer, and promoter of our wines," says Mrs. Kenneth Schuchter.

Wines of Valley Vineyards

Specialty Wines: Sangria and Honey (Mead).

WHITE WINE

Seyval Blanc, dry wine.
Ohio Sauterne, semi-dry villard blanc.
Niagara, semi-sweet.

RED WINE

Baco Noir, estate-bottled.
Blue Eye, limited, from a new American hybrid.
De Chaunac, estate-bottled.
Hillside Red, blend of hybrids.
Pink Catawba, sweet.
Pink Concord, sweet.
Valley Rosé, semi-dry.

Price of wines: $3.00-$4.00.

Vinterra Farm Winery and Vineyard
ESTABLISHED 1977

6505 Stoker Road, Houston, OH 45333

Phone: 513-492-2071

Owners, Homer K. and Phyllis Jean Monroe; sales manager, John Monroe.

Vineyards: 18 acres French hybrids.

Visiting: May 1-Nov. 1, Tuesday through Friday, 1:00 p.m.-10:00 p.m.; Saturday, 11:00 a.m.-7:00 p.m.; Nov. 1-May 1, Tuesday through Thursday, 5:00 p.m.-9:00 p.m.; Friday, 4:00 p.m.-10:00 p.m.; Saturday, 1:00 p.m.-11:00 p.m.

Storage capacity: 3,000 gallons.

Directions: Turn off Interstate 75 at Sidney, drive west on state route 47, 7 miles to Oran. Left at Oran on Dawson Road 2 miles. Left again on Stoker ¼ mile.

"The winery was Bud's idea," says Phyllis Jean Monroe. A former teacher of American literature, both high school and college levels, Mrs. Monroe gave up her teaching career to devote all her time to the winery. Her husband still holds a full-time position as vice-president of a corporation making industrial fans. His love for farming and his reading about the revival of winegrowing in Ohio were twin incentives for buying Vinterra Farm and clearing the land to plant vines.

Son John, as sales manager, is the third partner in this family enterprise. Linda, John's wife, welcomes visitors and helps with the party planning. "We want to keep Vinterra Farms Winery small. We don't want to grow bigger," the Monroes declare.

The eighteen acres of French hybrid grapes were planted in 1973, so the vines are now bearing, but the production so far is going into the blends for red, white, and rosé wines. Eventually, the Monroes will make varietal wines from these grapes. Aurora, seyval blanc, and villard blanc are the white grapes; baco, de Chaunac, and Chancellor are the hybrid reds growing at Vinterra. Catawba, Ohio's own native grape, has also been planted here.

There are 600 apple trees on the farm, so apple wine will join the grape wines one day, and a honey wine is also in the Monroe plans.

After fermentation in stainless steel, white wines are given some age in steel barrels, while red wines mature in small oak barrels.

Built in Bavarian style, the winery has a hospitality room, a meeting room where tastings and parties can be held, and a long veranda for fair weather wine sampling.

Vinterra winery is open all year except on Sundays and Mondays. Special parties can be arranged with a week's notice.

And, by the way, Houston is pronounced How-ston, not Hue-ston as in Texas.

Wines of Vinterra Farm

WHITE WINE

Catawba, sweet.
Chablis, dry, blend of French hybrids.
Niagara, dry.
Sauterne, sweet.

RED WINE

Claret, blend of hybrid grapes.
Burgundy, blend of hybrids.
Pink Chablis, medium dry.
Rosé, medium dry.
Concord, sweet.

Price of wines: All $2.75.

Wyandotte Wine Cellar, Inc.
ESTABLISHED 1976

4640 Wyandotte Drive, Gahanna, OH 43230

Phone: 614-476-3624

Owner, Floyd Jones.

Vineyards: None: Most fruits, all grapes purchased.

Visiting: Daily 10:00 a.m.-6:00 p.m.

Storage capacity: 10,000 gallons.

Directions: Close to Columbus. Take east branch of I-270 which circles Columbus, to Morse Road. Morse Road east to Cherry Bottom Road, left to Wyandotte Drive, and left on Wyandotte.

Floyd and Peggy Jones visited Iowa's Amana Colonies in 1974, and it was a turning point in their lives. When they tasted the rhubarb wine made in all of the tiny wineries, they loved it, and almost on the spot, Wyandotte Wine Cellar had its inception.

Soon after that, the Joneses tucked 600 baby rhubarb plants into their farmland soil, and in 1977 they made their first rhubarb wine. Soon thereafter, they began making other fruit wines—and even fermented dandelion blossoms and made grapefruit wine from juice brought from Florida, where they go every winter.

There are grape wines, as well. Concord and another native grape, the Ontario, are made into sweet varietal wines. Local growers provide French hybrids. With such bounty readily available, the Joneses don't see any point in planting a vineyard. Their customers are delighted with the many kinds of wine they find at Wyandotte Wine Cellar; it needn't all be homegrown.

Wines of Wyandotte Wine Cellar

Fruit wines including apple, blueberry, cherry, elderberry, grapefruit, peach, rhubarb, tomato, dandelion and red clover wines.

WHITE WINE

Ontario, semi-sweet.
Wyandotte White, dry, from French hybrid grapes.

RED WINE

Sweet Concord
Ohio Rosé, medium-dry.

Wyandotte Mellow Red, semi-sweet, blend of labrusca and French hybrids.
Wyandotte Burgundy, dry blend of labrusca and hybrid grapes.

Price of wines: $2.40-$3.85.

Several new Ohio wineries were entering the scene as we were going to press:

At Dover, Dalton (Duke) Bixler and Floyd Jones opened Der Marktplatz and Breitenbach Winery on Route 39, halfway between Dover and Sugar Creek. The location is in Ohio's Little Switzerland area where excellent cheese and sausage are made, and these products are available in the winery shop.

At Granville, Attorney Stanley J. Brockman produced a "practice" batch of wine, 450 gallons in all, and said he was not in a hurry to reach his goal of several thousand gallons. He wants to learn from his mistakes, he told us. He isn't certain that he won't change the name of his winery from Brockman to Granville, and until his half-acre of aurora, seyval, and Foch mature, he'll get all his grapes from Ken Schuchter of Valley Vineyards at Morrow.

At Madison, another winery is developing. Charles and Dana Daughters, father and son, were bonded late in 1980, as was Stanley Brockman. Dana had been working and was inspired by Bill Worthy of Grand River. The senior Daughters, Charles, purchased a flower shop to be converted into the winery. Grapes being planted are both hybrid and vinifera varieties, and, of course, the Daughters duo will buy their grapes until their own vines produce.

Christina
WINE CELLARS

Alc. 10% By Vol.

Natural Apple Wine

Table wine produced and bottled by
The Lawlor Family Winery

B.W.-WI.-28

This very special Apple Wine is made from carefully selected apples grown in Wisconsin's famous Kickapoo Valley located near Gays Mills, Wisconsin.

The apples are pressed, fermented, and aged under the watchful supervision of our Enologist and

Door Peninsula Winery

natural sweet

plum Wine

a natural plum table wine

Alcohol 12% by volume

Produced and Bottled by
DOOR PENINSULA WINE, INC.,
RT. 1, STURGEON BAY, WI. 54235   B.W. 25

STONE MILL

NATURAL
CHERRY
TABLE
WINE

750ML (25.4 FL OZ)

Produced and Bottled by
Stone Mill Winery, Inc.
Cedarburg, Wisconsin

Alc. 12% By Vol.

The Wines of Wisconsin

Wisconsin, the nation's number one beer producer, with nine big breweries (plus eight experimental breweries) on Uncle Tax-man's list, not only drinks a lot of beer,* but is America's next biggest brandy consumer. (California, the country's brandy-maker, consumes a tad more.)

So, why would anyone associate grapes or wine with Wisconsin? Cherry wineries, which also make cranberry and apple wine, seem natural, for they process indigenous crops. Delicious as some of these wines may be, they are "fruit" wines, most of them classed as "other than standard" because of the sugar that must be added to make them palatable. To a wine buff, they are not wine, for the classical definition of wine has to do with grapes alone.

The climate of Wisconsin is not a good one for grapes, with the exception of small pockets or microclimates which, because of some protection from the elements, such as the presence of a large body of water, or sloping hills that protect vines from the wind, permit grape vines to exist.

Such a microclimate, with hills and a broad river, permitted the establishment of Wisconsin's single grape winery, which is now making an impact among the wines of the Midwest. Wollersheim Winery, on

* About 5 million barrels annually.

Agoston Haraszthy's old stamping grounds, is Wisconsin's first, but probably not the last winery, as the state lays claim to several experimental vineyards.

Christina Wine Cellars
ESTABLISHED 1978

109 Vine Street, La Crosse, WI 54601

Phone: 608-785-2210

Proprietor, winemaker: Christine K. Lawlor.

Vineyards: None. Fruit wines, grape wines from California fruit.

Gift shop specializing in copper and brass; amateur winemaking supplies.

Hours: 10:00 a.m.-9:00 p.m. daily in summer. Sunday noon to 6:00 p.m.

Storage capacity: 35,000 gallons.

Directions: Downtown La Crosse, next to River Front Park.

We've met Christine Lawlor before—in McGregor, Iowa, you may recall. The young enologist was so successful in the Lawlor family's first winery that a second winery in an equally interesting, tourist-favored location was sought. An old freight house with tracks on both sides and four boxcars to turn into shops was the pot of gold at the end of this particular rainbow. Timothy Lawlor helps his sister handle facilities in both wineries.

Wines of Christina Wine Cellars

Fruit wines include apple, apple and cranberry, cherry.

WHITE WINE
Catawba
Chablis, from french hybrid grapes.
Niagara

RED WINE

Concord
Burgundy, from french hybrid grapes.
Port, from California grapes.

Price of wines: $3.25.

Door Peninsula Wine Company
ESTABLISHED 1974

Sturgeon Bay, WI 54235

Phone 715-483-9317

President, Evangeline Alberts; secretary-treasurer, Tom Alberts; wine-maker, Julius Alberts.

Vineyards: 6½ acres of hybrids (experimental).

Visiting: Daily 9:00 a.m.-5:00 p.m. May 1-December 31. Until 7:00 p.m. July 1-September 1. For off season hours, phone 715-743-7431. Guided tours. Cheese room.

Storage capacity: 10,000 gallons.

Directions: Highway 42, Carlsville (about 8 miles south of Egg Harbor).

Door County is one of the Midwest's favorite recreation areas.* Fishing, sailing, swimming, scuba diving, hiking, and horseback riding are favorite sports. In winter, cross country skiing and snowmobiling are enjoyed. The Door Peninsula winery is a delightful, relaxing place for all of these active people and for others who don't indulge in sports but love Door County for its beauty, history, cultural activities, and shops.

The winery is located in an 1868 schoolhouse. Winemaker Julius Alberts had been making wines for other Wisconsin fruit wineries for a

---

* I may be forgiven for mentioning that the current best guide to Door County is *Easy Going, A Comprehensive Guide to Door County*, by Charles F. Church (Tamarack Press). Church is a son of the author of *Wines of the Midwest*.

number of years when he decided to buy the schoolhouse and start his own winery. With seventeen years of winemaking to his credit, he's the veteran of Wisconsin winemakers. The Alberts planted a vineyard, in May of 1975, with wines from hybrid grapes in mind, but the winter of 1976-77 took a great toll and it will be a few years before grape wines can be offered. The fruit wines are made of Door County fruits.

The winery is situated on an acre of land with picnic tables scattered about, where guests may sip wine and munch Wisconsin cheese, which is also sold there.

Wines of Door Peninsula Winery

Apple, dry or sweet.
Cherry, dry or sweet.
Pear, dry or sweet.
Plum, dry or sweet.

Price of wines: About $2.60.

Fruit of the Woods Wine Cellar, Inc.
ESTABLISHED 1972

1113 Wall Street, Eagle River, WI 54521

Phone: 715-479-4800

President, John McCain; secretary-treasurer, Maureen McCain; vice president and winemaker, Scott McCain.

Vineyards: None. Fruit and berry wines.

Visiting: 9:00-5:00 daily all year. Tours May 1-December 31. Gift shop. Cranberry wine cheese.

Storage capacity: 9,000 gallons.

Directions: In the town of Eagle River. Not hard to find. . . .   follow the crowd!

John McCain tells us that winter hours are going to depend, to some extent, upon the weather. The winery was open all winter in 1978 and 1979, but the disastrous snows of early 1979 kept the usual throngs of winter sports buffs locked in Chicago. Eagle River and environs are popular with sports fans the year around.

The McCains' son, Scott, has taken over the winemaking from his father.

Wines of Fruit of the Woods Wine Cellar

Apricot (dried fruit).
Cherry, from fresh fruit.
Cranberry, local crop.
Wild plum, local.
Raspberry, from frozen fruit.
Strawberry, from frozen fruit.
Cabernet sauvignon, from California.

Price of wines: $3.00-$3.50. A "baker's dozen" if you buy a case.

Stone Mill Winery, Inc.

ESTABLISHED 1971

N. 70 W6340 E. Bridge Road, Cedarburg, WI 53012

Phone: 414-377-8020

President and treasurer, James B. Pape; vice president-secretary, Sandra Pape.

Vineyards: None. Cherry wine.

Visiting: Daily tours all year (50¢; under 18 no charge). Monday-Saturday 10:00 a.m.-5:00 p.m.; Sunday noon-5:00 p.m.

Storage capacity: 30,000 gallons.

Directions: 95 miles from Chicago. Cedarburg is just north of Milwaukee on state Highway 57. Once there, you can't miss the winery.

The old stone building that houses Stone Mill Winery was a woolen mill for nearly a hundred years before it was vacated, in 1967. The wine made there comes from Door County cherries, and may be bought in ceramic bottles or in conventional glass. The winery itself has a lot of old fashioned charm, and so do the little shops and eating places in Cedarburg that have been recreated as turn-of-the-century establishments.

Wines of Stone Mill

Newberry Dry Hard Cider, Natural Cherry, Honey Cherry, Colonial Spice wines.

WHITE WINE
American White Grape Wine, dry.

RED WINE
American Red Grape Wine, semi-dry.

Price of wines: $2.69-$3.49.

Von Stiehl Wine, Inc.
ESTABLISHED 1963

P.O. Box 45, 115 Navarino St., Algoma, WI 54201. Other premises, Baraboo.

Phone: 414-487-5208

Owner, Von Stiehl Wine, Inc.; president, C.W. Stiehl; general manager, Don Atkins.

No vineyard. Cherry and apple wines.

Visiting: May 1-January 1, 9:00 a.m.-5:00 p.m. every day. Free tours.

Storage capacity: 54,000 gallons.

Directions: First street south of the river, east on Navarino Street to 115. In Baraboo, follow signs for Circus World Museum. It's across the street.

Proprietor Stiehl is a medical doctor, who used to wrap his bottles of cherry wine in cheesecloth "bandages" to resemble a leg in a cast. The unique wrap kept out light while the wine aged, but like the stone crock once used for other wines, it has been abandoned; the modern substitute is a grainy white or black paint. The wrapped bottle was impractical, though attractive and amusing. It's a collector's bottle now.

Von Stiehl wines are made of Door County's famous Montmorency cherries without water or preservatives. They come both dry and sweet.

The winery at Algoma was a 100-year-old brewery which Dr. Stiehl restored. Visitors are shown the old rathskeller where wines are fermented, and the salon upstairs, which is decorated with French tapestries and Austrian artifacts donated by the Prince of Liechtenstein. Dr. Stiehl represents the wines of the tiny principality which are available at both the Algoma and Baraboo wineries.

Crown Prince Hans Adam Pius of Liechtenstein conferred the title of *Graf* (count) on Dr. Stiehl in making him consul for Liechtenstein.

The winery at Baraboo is another old brewery, some of its walls two-and-a-half feet thick, filled with a foot-thick layer of cork for insulation. Its decor resembles that of the Algoma winery, with artifacts from Liechtenstein lending a European flavor. There is a patio garden where people can sit with wine and the cheese spread made by the winery.

The special cheese, apple and cherry jellies are sold at both wineries. Personalized labels may be ordered for the wines.

Baraboo is the home of the Circus World Museum (it was the original home of the Ringling and Gollmar circuses). There are daily performances, parades, animal shows and calliope music all summer long.

The Baraboo area is geologically interesting because of its "Baraboo Alps," a worn-down range of quartzite mountains millions of years old.

Wines of Von Stiehl

Dry Cherry Wine
Sweet Cherry Wine
Dry Apple Wine
Sweet Apple Wine

Price of wines: About $3.00; $3.50 for the painted bottle.

Wisconsin Winery

ESTABLISHED 1979

529 Main Street, Lake Geneva, WI 53147

Phone: 414-248-3245

Proprietors, winemakers, Bud and Arlene Brenton.

Vineyards: None. Fruit and berry wines from Wisconsin and other midwestern states.

Amateur winemaking supplies, gift shop.

Visiting: 10:00 a.m.-5:00 p.m. year around. Tours and tasting, every half hour. Closed Monday, Tuesday.

Storage capacity: 25,000 gallons.

Directions: At junction of Highway 50 and County Road H.

Lake Geneva is an active town the year around, with summer and winter sports: sailing, ice boating, fishing, skiing and other fun. The Brentons, like many others, fell into commercial winemaking by way of making their own wines at home. Their winery was built as a typewriter factory in 1887 and has metamorphosed many times; once into a boatmaking company, another time into a bus depot. You'll hear all about it as you tour and taste.

Wines of Wisconsin Winery

Apricot, cranberry, elderberry, pear, plum, strawberry and raspberry.

Price of wines: $4.50. Raspberry, $5.50.

The Wollersheim Winery, Inc.

ESTABLISHED 1972

Highway 188, Prairie du Sac, WI 53578

Phone: 608-643-6515

President, winemaker, Robert P. Wollersheim; secretary, JoAnn Wollersheim.

Vineyards: 20 acres French hybrids and vinifera.

Winemaking supplies, nursery stock, estate wines, California and European wines.

Visiting: Daily, all year, 10:00 a.m.-5:00 p.m. Tour with tasting, $1.00; children under 11, no charge. Tasting and picnicking on grounds, no charge.

Storage capacity: 18,000 gallons.

Directions: 2½ miles north of Highway 12 on Highway 188; or ½ mile south of Prairie du Sac bridge on 188.

Few Americans have ever set eyes on that rare bird, the American bald eagle. But if you visit the Wollersheim Winery in winter, you'll see thirty or forty eagles soaring over the winery, the hills, and the Wisconsin River. You won't see them in summer, but you can picnic on the grounds, see the old winery built by Peter Kehl in 1867, and vineyards first planted by Agoston Haraszthy, the "father" of California viticulture, who tried for two years to grow wine grapes here before he sold out and took off in 1848, for the West.

Bob and JoAnn Wollersheim, and their three youngsters, lucked-out when they found the winery and the seventeen-room farmhouse, which they bought in 1972. They had much work to do to make the old farmhouse (without central heating or electricity) livable and the winery operative, after the vines were planted. Bob bought grapes from Pennsylvania to make his early wines.

He was then program manager of a space study of the planet Venus, in the Space Science and Engineering Center at the University of Wisconsin, Madison, twenty-five minutes away. Bob still is there, but now teaches half-time, for he believes that "it is physically impossible to lead two lives." His major interest has more to do with good old planet Earth.

When you visit the Wollersheim Winery, you'll see the cave where Peter Kehl lived while building the winery and farmhouse. Bob and JoAnn believe that Haraszthy first tunneled into the hill, and that an old bottle of wine which they found may have been his. Haraszthy kept the crop rights when he sold out, and they theorize that he may have come back to make some wine. The bottle was dated 1853. It's an interesting speculation. More is known about Peter Kehl, however.

Kehl made altar and table wines of native American grapes which could survive the rugged winters, while Haraszthy's vinifera varieties could not. Kehl's son, Jacob, succeeded him, and shipped wines to Chicago and Milwaukee by horse and cart. The Kehls used the upper floor of the winery for a dance hall. In 1899, Jacob died without knowing that even his native grapes had frozen in the bitterest winter in Wisconsin history. The next two generations of Kehls farmed, using the winery for a barn.

There was plenty of wine in the cellars when Prohibition came along, and the Wollersheims have the license that permitted the Kehls to hold an all-day sale before the cellars were closed. They learned from old newspaper clippings that people came from miles around to haul the wine away, and that the sale turned into a drunken revel with inebriated people falling downhill. After all, it was the last day to drink!

The Wollersheims have recently visited Germany and returned full of excitement about planting a cornfield to white riesling. After talking with leading authorities of German viticulture, they are convinced that their Wisconsin hills have the right soil and climate conditions for riesling. They also grow some chardonnay.

Wollersheim Winery will have a hand-carved cask to mark each year of vintage. The casks are large Spanish puncheons. Tony Dunn of Prairie du Sac designs them and the carving is done by another local artist, Bill Wilkie of Cross Plains.

Wines of Wollersheim Winery

There are changes from year to year as more grapes come into production.

WHITE WINE

Aurore Blanc
Seyval Blanc
Sugarloaf White, oak-aged blend of aurore, seyval and riesling.

RED WINE

Baco Noir, (100 percent)
Baco Noir Nouveau ($^2/_3$ baco, $^1/_3$ Foch)

Chelois
De Chaunac
Landot
Leon Millot

Price of wines: $3.50-$5.00.

Friends and
Neighbors

Sometimes it is difficult to tell where the Midwest leaves off and the South, or East, of the United States begins.

With apologies to Arkansas' nine other wineries, we are going to bring Wiederkehr Wine Cellars into the Midwestern fold, first because Wiederkehr has good Midwestern distribution and is a name well-known among the wineries of the United States. Second, because the Wiederkehrs are so actively working on wines from better-than-native grapes. And third, because the winery and its restaurant are a delight to tourists from all over the Midwest.

In addition, we'd enjoy conducting readers on a tour of Lake Erie wineries in Pennsylvania and New York, for the reason that it's so natural to follow the grape trail eastward after looking in on Ohio's wineries at Madison and Conneaut. Ever so quickly we find ourselves in North East, Pennsylvania (oddly, North East is located in *northwest* Pennsylvania!) where four wineries await our inspection. Just a few miles farther east, along the shores of the Big Lake, we cross into New York's Chautauqua County, home of another four wineries, two of them newly ready to challenge our faltering palates.

All of these establishments—Ohio's, Pennsylvania's and New York's —lie close to the southern shores of Lake Erie and thus qualify for a federal Lake Erie wine district designation; they may achieve it in the early 1980s.

Is Arkansas Midwestern? Well, yes!

Wiederkehr Wine Cellars, Inc.
ESTABLISHED 1880

RR 1, Box 14, Altus, AR 72821

Phone: 501-468-2611 or 468-3611

Owners, the Wiederkehr family; board chairman, Alcuin Wiederkehr; president, Leo Wiederkehr.

Vineyards: 575 acres vinifera, hybrids, native grapes.

Visiting: Monday-Saturday 9:00 a.m.-4:30 p.m.

Restaurant: Wiederkehr Chalet Suisse Wein Keller Restaurant.

Gift Shop.

Storage capacity: 1,750,000 gallons.

Directions: If you can find Altus on U.S. Highway 64, you can find St. Mary's Mountain. Drive on up to Wiederkehr.

Wiederkehr is a winery, a restaurant, a gift shop, a cooper's shop, a small mountain, and much of the town of Altus. The estate comprises 2,800 acres, but as Alcuin Wiederkehr, chairman of the family corporation, says, "You can see that a lot of it is cliffs and rocks." A lot of it is vineyards, too, 100 acres of the 575 planted to vinifera varieties of classical wine grapes. These vines produce gold medal-winning wines.

The winery is a Swiss chalet. You are almost in Switzerland in this environment, so eager are the Wiederkehrs to preserve their family heritage. You wouldn't believe how much a family corporation this is. Al's parents, retired from their winemaking chores, operate the gift shop in this Arkansas Swiss village. Brother Leo manages the restaurant, while sister Dolores presides at the bar. Dolores' husband, Don

Neumeier, is production manager. When I lunched with the Wieder-kehrs in their restaurant, our waitress was Leo's pretty daughter, Bren-da. During lunch, host Al Wiederkehr, spotting another brother's wife at a nearby table, leaped to his feet with joyful greeting. The young woman was with several friends having a last luncheon get-together before school would be out and their freedom curtailed for the summer.

That isn't all there is to say about Wiederkehr relatives. Grandpa John Andrew Wiederkehr came from Switzerland to establish this winery. He had a sister, whose descendants operate three other winer-ies at Altus: Post Winery, Inc., at the foot of St. Mary's Mountain (Wiederkehr is at the top), Mt. Bethel Winery, and Henry J. Sax winery.

Al Wiederkehr, who is chief executive officer as well as chairman of the corporation, is a graduate of Notre Dame. He persuaded authori-ties there to let him keep a case of wine sent him by his father, Her-man, despite a ban on alcoholic drink in the dorms. He went from Notre Dame to California to study viticulture and enology, then to Bordeaux as an exchange student, for ten months. He also spent time with Konstantin Frank, New York's famous grower of classical grapes. Given this background and Al's determination, there may be some great wines out of Arkansas yet. You get the feeling that if the climate proved too warm for certain famous grapes, Al Wiederkehr would air condition his mountain.

Wines of Wiederkehr

Sparkling wines, sherries, ports, fruit wines.

WHITE WINE

Chardonnay
Chenin Blanc
Gewürztraminer
Vin Blanc Sec
Sauvignon Blanc
Swiss Chalet (dry house wine).
Catawba
Niagara
Delaware

RED WINE

Baco Noir
Cabernet Sauvignon
Zinfandel
Cynthiana, (native Arkansas grape).
Alpine Rosé
Pinot Noir
Many others.

Price of wines: $2.79-$6.79.

Lake Erie Wineries of Pennsylvania

Heritage Wine Cellars
ESTABLISHED 1978

12162 East Main Road, North East, PA 16428

Phone: 814-725-8015

Partners: Bostwick brothers, Robert C., Michael N., William M. (winemaker); business manager-consultant, Kenneth Bostwick (father).

Vineyards: 400 acres, mostly for juice operation. Wine grapes purchased from growers on contract.

Visiting: Daily 10:00 a.m.-6:00 p.m. Summer weekends, open until 9:00 p.m. Open Sundays as soon as state law permits, same hours.

Storage capacity: Wine only, 8,000 gallons; including juice 1,000,000 gallons.

Directions: State line exit from I-90. "You can't miss it!" Big silo juice tanks visible for miles from I-90. Winery is 50 yards from exit.

Heritage has a special meaning for the Bostwick brothers, whose great-great-grandfather, Dewitt Clinton Bostwick, bought the family farm 180 years ago, and founded the family business, the Great Lakes Juice Company, of which the winery is an offshoot. The brothers own the wine business, but they say their father is the moving force behind the project.

Visitors marvel at the "cellars" converted from a big barn built in the late 1800's. Its stone walls give you the feeling of being underground. The structure has hand-hewn beams all in one piece and more than seventy feet long.

Wines of Heritage Wine Cellars

WHITE WINE

Catawba
Chablis (hybrid blend).
Rhine (hybrid blend).
Seyval Blanc
Delaware
Niagara
Sweet Country White (blended hybrids and labrusca).

RED WINE

Concord
Isabella (native grape).
Sweet Rosé (concord and delaware).
Burgundy (hybrid blend).

Price of wines: $2.50-$3.10.

Mazza Vineyards, Inc.
ESTABLISHED 1972

11815 East Lake Road, North East, PA 16428

Phone: 814-725-8695

President-general manager, Robert Mazza; secretary-treasurer, Joseph Mazza; winemakers, Frank Mazza, Gary Mosier.

Vineyards: 2 acres. Most grapes are purchased.

Visiting: Tours and sales, June-September 9:00 a.m.-9:00 p.m. daily except Sunday. October-May, close at 5:30, except for Friday and Saturday, when open till 9:00.

Tasting room, gift shop.

Storage capacity: 50,000 gallons.

Directions: 2 miles east of North East on Rt. 5.

Mazza is more than ever a family business since former winemaker Helmut Kranich returned to his native Germany, in 1978, to become general manager of the famous Schloss Eltz. It was a trade-off, one might say, as Frank Mazza returned from army duty in Germany to take over the winemaking responsibility, with the help of Kranich-trained Gary Mosier.

Robert and Frank Mazza carry on the day-to-day operation of the winery. Their father, Joseph, keeps the records. Wines are made of the better native grapes, Pennsylvania-grown vinifera varieties and hybrids. Though Mazza white wines have a fine reputation, the Mazzas are increasing their emphasis on red wines. There are two "extension of premises" operations, in Erie and Pittsburgh.

In December 1979 Mazza Vineyards merged with Mt. Hope Estate and Winery of Lancaster, PA. The two wineries maintain their separate identities as subsidiaries of Spirited, Inc., located at Mount Hope.

Wines of Mazza

Apple wine, Champagne (chardonnay).

WHITE WINE

Delaware, semi-sweet.
Dutchess, semi-sweet.
Mazza White Wine, dry.

RED WINE

Baco Noir

Cabernet Sauvignon
Chelois
De Chaunac
Gamay
Light Red Concord
Catawba Rosé, semi-sweet.
Steuben Rosé, dry.
Sweet Rosé

Price of wines: $2.60-$4.00. Champagne $8.50.

Penn-Shore Vineyards, Inc.
ESTABLISHED 1969

10225 East Lake Road, North East, PA 16428

Phone: 814-725-9422

Officers: President, Philip B. McCord; vice president, George F. Luke; secretary-treasurer, George W. Sceiford; general manager-winemaker, David B. Thiebeau.

Vineyards: 125 acres.

Visiting: 9:00 a.m.-9:00 p.m. daily except Sunday, May through December. Same hours Fridays and Saturdays rest of year, but closed at 5:30 other days.

Storage capacity: 175,000 gallons.

Directions: On SR-5, three miles northwest of North East.

Penn-Shore is Pennsylvania's biggest winery. Its founders, along with Douglas Moorhead of Presque Isle, and several others, were influential in getting the state's Limited Winery Act passed in 1968. That was the beginning of the growth of small wineries in the state. The act limits production to 100,000 gallons a year; Penn-Shore produces about half that amount, but its storage capacity is greater.

Penn-Shore wines are available through state stores, a victory of sorts. Pennsylvania exercises strict control of sales, even though it is an important wine-growing state. The restraint of free enterprise is onerous for its wineries.

Wines of Penn-Shore Vineyards

Bottle-fermented champagne, sparkling burgundy.

WHITE WINE

Catawba, sweet.
Delaware, semi-dry.
Dutchess, dry.
Seyval Blanc, dry.
Vidal Blanc, dry.
Kir, white wine with black currant liqueur.

RED WINE

Baco Noir, dry.
Ruby Cascade, semi-sweet.
Concord, sweet.
Dry Red
Foch, dry.
Pennsylvania Red, dry.
Pennsylvania Rosé, semi-sweet.
Pink Catawba, sweet.
Sangria, red wine with fruit juices.

Price of wines: $2.50-$3.00. Sparkling, $6.00.

Presque Isle Wine Cellars

ESTABLISHED 1964

9440 Buffalo Rd., North East, PA 16428

Phone: 814-725-1314

Co-owners, Douglas P. Moorhead, Marlene B. Moorhead.

Vineyards: 20 acres. Grapes also bought wholesale from cousin John Moorhead's extensive vineyards.

Visiting: Tuesday-Saturday, 8:00 a.m.-5:00 p.m. Sundays 8:00 a.m.-2:30 p.m. in fresh juice season.

Winery equipment, supplies for amateur winemakers.

Storage capacity: 10,000 gallons.

Directions: *Westbound* on I-90, take Exit 12 (State Line Exit) west on Rt. 20, 6½ miles. *Eastbound* Exit 10, north on Rt. 531 to U.S. 20. Right on 20 four miles.

The Douglas Moorheads live in Moorheadville, in the ancestral mansion that was an old stagecoach-stop lodging house built in 1837. Douglas' father was president of Welch Grape Juice Company. Their winery is full of French hybrid and vinifera varietal wines and also winemaking equipment of all kinds, which they sell. They sell large quantities of juice to amateur winemakers in season, and they give a lot of practical advice free. Order Presque Isle's free catalog listing supplies and books available.

Wines of Presque Isle

WHITE WINE

Chardonnay
Delaware
Dutchess
Seyval Blanc
White Riesling
Vidal Blanc

RED WINE

Cabernet Sauvignon
Chambourcin
Chancellor
De Chaunac
Gamay

Price of wines: $2.20-$5.50 (Cabernet Sauvignon).

Lake Erie Wineries of New York

Chadwick Bay Wine Company
ESTABLISHED 1980

10001 Rt. 60, Fredonia, N.Y. 14063

Phone:

Partners: George Borzilleri, Richard Mazza; winemaker, Eric Miller.

Vineyards: None, grapes purchased.

Visiting: Monday-Saturday 10:00 a.m.-5:00 p.m., Sunday noon-5:00 p.m.

Storage capacity: 31,000 gallons.

Directions: Exit 59 from I-90 brings you to Rt. 60. Left on 60, 1½ miles. On your right.

In late 1980 Chadwick Bay Wine Company was nearly ready to join the three other Chautauqua-Lake Erie area wineries in producing premium quality New York State wines, the first, a Nouveau Red, launched before Christmas. Eric Miller, son of Mark and Dene Miller of Benmarl Vineyards and formerly the family's winemaker, helped design and equip the Chadwick Bay winery and reports enthusiastically that the company will specialize in premium wines from the better hybrids, plans to "grow big" and to market out of state as well as within New York boundaries. An annual spring wine festival is planned.

Wines of Chadwick Bay Wine Company

WHITE WINE

Chardonnay
Seyval Blanc

Vidal Blanc
Spring Wine, fresh, fruity, slightly sweet.

RED WINE

Chambourcin
Classic New Yorker
Dry Rosé
Rosé Demi-sec

Price of wines: $3.50-$5.50.

Frederick S. Johnson Vineyards
ESTABLISHED 1962

West Main Road, P.O. Box 52, Westfield, NY 14787

Phone: 716-326-2191

Owner, Frederick S. Johnson; manager-winemaker, William A. Gulvin.

Vineyards: 135 acres native and hybrid grapes.

Visiting: Monday-Friday, 9:00 a.m.-noon; Saturday 9:00 a.m.-noon. Closed Sunday.

Tours in July and August only.

Storage capactiy: 75,000 gallons.

Directions: On Route 20, 2 miles west of Westfield.

Frederick Johnson's background as an agricultural expert includes work with the Dole Company in Hawaii, and fourteen years developing and managing the Rockefeller plantations in Venezuela. Since 1961, he has taken over his family's vineyards, in the Chautauqua district of New York, where he is consistently replacing concord vines with the best of French-American hybrids for the area.

Wines of Frederick S. Johnson

WHITE WINE

Aurora Blanc, dry.
Delaware, semi-dry.
White Wine, semi-dry (seyval, aurora, delaware blend).
Seyval Blanc, dry.
Liebestropfchen ("little love drops," all delaware).

RED WINE

Chancellor Noir, dry.
Ives Noir, semi-sweet.
Cascade Rouge, dry, sold only at the winery.
Robust Red, dry, sold only at the winery.
Cascade Rosé, dry.

All wines are 100 percent New York State.

Price of wines: $3.99-$4.99.

Merritt Estate Winery
ESTABLISHED 1976

2264 King Road, Forestville, N.Y. 14062

Phone: 716-965-4800

President, general manager, winemaker, William T. Merritt; vice president, Alfred J. Sample; treasurer, Marguerite K. Sample.

Vineyards: 70 acres; 30 additional acres leased.

Tasting room, picnic facilities, box lunches for groups arriving by bus.

Visiting: All year, daily 10:00-a.m.-5:00 p.m.; Sunday, 1 p.m.-5:00 p.m.

Storage capacity: 24,000 gallons.

Directions: Leave I-90 at Exit 58. Go west on Rt. 20 to first flashing light in Sheridan Center. Left at light. Follow signs.

The Merritt Estate is a farm that has been in Bill Merritt's mother Marguerite Sample's family since 1890. Originally the property was devoted to general agriculture, including a dairy farm. Some grapes were grown, but not until 1960 did grapes become a specialty.

"We're very heavy in the French hybrids," says Bill, whose wife Christi, mother, and step-father, Alfred Sample, are all active participants in the vineyard and winery operations. Two native grapes are grown, niagara, for a popular wine, and some catawba; no other native grapes are cultivated. Neither do the Merritts plan to grow any vinifera grapes. "It's more practical to do what we're good at, producing premium quality New York State wines," Bill Merritt says. The company has good distribution in the state.

Wines of Merritt Estate Winery

Chautauqua series of red and white blended sweet and semi-sweet wines.

WHITE WINE

Aurora Blanc
Niagara
Seyval Blanc
Sheridan White Wine

RED WINE

Baco Noir
De Chaunac
Maréchal Foch
Sheridan Red Wine

Price of wines: $3.29-$4.35.

Woodbury Vineyards
ESTABLISHED 1979

R.D. 1, South Roberts Road, Dunkirk, NY 14048

Phone: 716-679-1708

President, Gary F. Woodbury; winemaker, Andrew Z. Dabrowski.

Vineyards: 30 acres native, hybrids, vinifera.

Visiting: Tours and tastings daily, all year: 10:00 a.m.-5:00 p.m., Sunday, 1:00 p.m.-5:00 p.m.

Gift shop, amateur winemaking supplies.

Storage capacity: 20,000 gallons.

Directions: Exit 59, New York State Throughway, left on Rt. 60, left again on 20, right on South Roberts Road.

Gary and Bob Woodbury and Bob's wife Page are carrying on old Woodbury family tradition as grape growers. The Woodbury brothers are the fourth generation of grape farmers, but the first to establish a winery. "We grow everything!" exclaims Gary. "Native grapes, French hybrids and vinifera. We're Chautauqua County's largest producers of vinifera."

When the Woodbury Winery was opened in the summer of 1980, wines were available from all three types of grapes, and the Woodburys were coddling three sparkling wines which would be ready to market by Christmas of '81. They are a blended white, a 100 percent *blanc de blancs* (chardonnay), and De Chaunac.

Before they became winemakers themselves, the Woodburys provided grapes for premium wines made by other small wineries in the area.

Wines of Woodbury Vineyards

WHITE WINE

Catawba
Chardonnay

Gewürztraminer
Niagara
Seyval Blanc
White Riesling

RED WINE

Cabernet Sauvignon
De Chaunac
Pinot Noir

Price of wines: From native grapes, $4.00; hybrids, $3.75-$4.00; vinifera, $6.75-$7.00.

The Cheeses
of the Midwest

Americans are cheese eaters. We increased our munching in the five years from 1971 to 1976 from 11.8 pounds per capita to 15.65. Then, nibbling steadily onward like battalions of hungry mice, we reached a yearly portion of 17.03 pounds per person in 1979. Total cheese production in 1979 was a hefty 3.8 billion pounds. That's a mountain of cheese by anybody's calculator!

Increased wine consumption may have helped, for wine and cheese are being served together all across the country. Many wineries offer visitors tastes of cheese as well as wine. The cheese tray is fashionable when wine is served at home. Also, cheese is usually served with wine as one of the many courses in dinner menus of wining and dining societies. However, the jump in consumption of cheese may have more to do with the greater consumption of pizzas, cheeseburgers, and lasagne in our country than with the trend toward pairing two of nature's best gifts to man, fermented grapes and curdled milk.

Most traditional kinds of cheese are made in the Midwest. Few were invented here. Even Colby, sometimes thought to be uniquely American, is simply a moister, softer, milder form of England's cheddar. First made in Colby, Wisconsin, its popularity spread, and this form of cheddar is sometimes called after other towns where it is popular. Colby is *Pinconning* in Michigan, for example.

We make more "Swiss" cheese than the Swiss, who, in self-defense, now label their original product *Switzerland Swiss*. About the only kind of European cheese we haven't copied is France's famous *chevre*, the tangy, soft, fresh cheese made wherever there are goats in France. In our country the few cheeses made of goat's milk go to the health food market; most of them are not very good.

All of the cheeses on the following list are made in the United States. The kinds to accompany wine are a matter of personal preference, although there are some guidelines. Midwestern wines offer a whole new spectrum of tastes to match with cheese, and that makes each wine and cheese party an adventure.

Kinds of Cheese made in the Midwest

American: Cheddar type. Usually mild-flavored pasteurized process blend of different lots of cheddar, colby, or washed curd, or a mixture of these. "Pasteurized process" indicates that the mixture was ground with emulsifier added, then heated enough to blend and pasteurize. It keeps well, makes a good cheeseburger-topper, or sandwich. It's a useful cooking cheese, but natural cheddar is preferred for wine.

Blue: The good moldy cheese that resembles French Roquefort but is made of cow's milk, not sheep's milk like the French product. Best blue cheeses have a well-developed mold throughout. A wine partner needs to be a robust red to cope with blue's distinctive flavor. Italian gorgonzola, English Stilton and Danish blue cheeses are in this category.

Brick: American original first made by John Jossie, a Swiss immigrant, in Dodge County, Wisconsin in 1876. Mild to moderately sharp in flavor, and medium soft in texture. When aged and sharp, it tends to be somewhat smelly. Better with wine if not smelly! Good with white wine, as well as red.

Brie: Soft, creamy cheese that "runs" when fully ripe and warmed at room temperature for serving. Edible white crust with brownish "threads" in it. Cheese must be eaten before it becomes overripe and nearly liquid. Crust becomes ammoniated at this stage. A marvelous cheese for the finest red wines. Of French origin.

Camembert: Of French origin, similar to Brie but usually of smaller size. Thin, edible crust; soft, creamy interior quickly goes "over the hill" when perfect ripeness is achieved.

Cheddar: Almost everyone's favorite cheese. Born in England, the firm cheese has developed well in the United States, particularly in Wisconsin and New York. In Wisconsin it is colored, in New York it usually is not. Well-aged cheddar (more than 2 years) tends to be sharp-flavored and to have a crumbly texture. Better for wine when not more than 1½ to 2 years old.

Colby: An American original variation on cheddar, developed in Colby, Wisconsin in 1885 by a 16-year-old cheese-maker, Joe Steinwand, whose father, Ambrose Steinwand, built a factory there in 1882. Softer, more open-textured, and usually milder than cheddar, it is a popular Midwestern cheese.

Cream: American original; soft, smooth-textured white cheese of delicate, slightly acidic flavor, it usually comes foil-wrapped in 3-ounce or 8-ounce packages under Kraft or Borden label. First made by W.A. Lawrence in Chester, New York in 1872. His factory was purchased by a company that later became part of Borden. For cheesecake, appetizers; not particularly suited to wine except possibly in canapes.

Curds: Pieces of fresh, unpressed cheese with the whey removed. Many cheese factories and cheese shops sell fresh curds, a delicious wine-hour snack. Freeze them if you can't eat immediately. They tend to become rubbery.

Edam: Mellow, nutty-flavored cheese of medium-firm texture that comes in a ball coated with red wax. Originated in Holland. A very good wine cheese.

Feta: Greek white cheese, a bit firmer than cream cheese. Made of goat's milk, so it has the typical slightly acidic flavor. Good in salads but not particularly suitable for wine.

Gouda: Looks like a flattened Edam in its red wax coat. Semi-soft to smooth, firm texture, often with small holes. Mellow nutty flavor. A Holland type cheese, excellent with wine.

Liederkranz: Creamy, strong-flavored cheese somewhat resembling limburger. A smelly cheese, better with beer than wine. Created in Monroe, New York by Emil Frey in 1892, it is now made only by the Borden Company.

Limburger: Of Belgian origin, rectangular shape, creamy texture. Strong flavor, strong smell when ripe. Catch it early and cold if you want it with wine, but it's better with beer! Genuine limburger aficionados enjoy it older, strong and smelly!

Monterey Jack: American original created in Monterey, California in 1892 by a family named Jacks. A semi-soft cheese good with wine. There's also a dry Sonoma Jack cheese, good for grating.

Mozzarella: Italian-type pizza cheese, mild in flavor and plastic in texture. For other Italian dishes, also. Really the same cheese as scamorze. Becomes stringy if heated too much. Not a wine cheese by itself.

Muenster: Mellow, semi-soft cheese with fine holes or eyes. Nutty flavor. A very good cheese to serve with wine.

Parmesan: Sharp, distinctive flavor. A hard, grating cheese used lavishly in Italian cookery. Not a cheese for wine.

Pinconning: In Michigan, a term for Colby cheese made in Pinconning.

Port du Salut: A Wisconsin cheese company (Purity) has the exclusive right to make this French cheese in the U.S.A. Semi-soft, mellow to robust in flavor, an excellent cheese to serve with wine.

Provolone: Firm, salty, smoky cheese, mellow to sharp in flavor. Comes bound with cord in pear, salami shapes. Good with robust red wine.

Ricotta: Soft, bland, fresh, moist white cheese for lasagne and other Italian dishes. When its curd is pressed and dried, the cheese can be grated. Not a wine cheese.

Romano: Italian type of cheese for grating. Sharp, piquant flavor, granular texture. Not the best choice for wine.

Scamorze: Another name for mozzarella, the pizza cheese.

Swiss: The cheese with the big holes. With its mild, sweet, nutty flavor, it's a good friend to wine. First factory founded in Green County, Wisconsin in 1869 by Nick Gerbes.

How to Appreciate Wine and Cheese

Make your own rules, if you have confidence in your own good judgment. Or follow these suggestions.

1. Cheese tastes best at room temperature. Red wine should be cool, white wine cold but not icy.
2. Smelly cheeses are usually better with beer than with wine.
3. Bread or crackers with cheese and wine should be plain, not seedy or salty; and let's forget about butter. Don't serve pickles, or anything else sharp in flavor. Fruit is nice, if you want some other food. Sausage, if not overloaded with garlic or pepper, is fine.
4. You need robust red wine to match a blue cheese or aged cheddar. A delicate white wine would be overwhelmed.
5. A cheese platter is often a good idea when you are serving wines. Choose different types of cheese, for example, a firm cheddar about 1½ years old, a semi-soft cheese such as port du salut, and a soft, crusted cheese such as brie or camembert. Garnish the platter with clusters of fresh grapes, slices of pear or apple.

How to Care for Cheese

It is usually not advisable to buy cheese in larger portions than can be consumed within a reasonable time. While most cheeses may be frozen, some of them (cream cheeses, for example) lose their attractive texture and become crumbly. Others, such as the blue-veined cheeses, can develop a soapy flavor in the freezer.

Cheddar and Swiss freeze well, but should be frozen only in small portions of not more than an inch in thickness.

Most cheese keeps fairly well in the refrigerator over several months, if well wrapped in foil or plastic. When molds grow on the surface, they may be scraped away without any harm to the cheese.

Brie, camembert, limburger and other soft-ripening cheeses should be purchased within their time limits of freshness and creaminess.

Choose them with care and in consultation with your cheese supplier as to the time they'll be at the point of perfect eating quality. It takes a Liederkranz cheese twenty-five days to ripen fully, at refrigerator temperature. Camembert usually reaches its perfect quality in four weeks from the time it leaves the cheese factory.

Except for cream and cottage cheese, room temperature is the right temperature for eating. Usually, it takes about two hours for cheese to warm sufficiently. If you can estimate the appetites, it is better to remove only the amount you'll eat from the refrigerator. Cheese doesn't improve with being alternately warmed and chilled.

The Cheeses
of Illinois

Because Wisconsin, its neighbor to the north, is the biggest cheese producer in the country, Illinois could get along nicely consuming Wisconsin cheese. But the Land of Lincoln has several claims to cheese fame of its own, especially at Lena, Nauvoo and Walnut.

The cheese factories we shall describe sell mail order cheese, so even if your favorite cheese store doesn't carry these fine cheeses, it is possible to sample them or serve them with the good wines of the Midwest.

Avanti Foods,
Walnut Cheese Division

P.O. Box 456, 109 Depot St., Walnut, IL 61376

Phone: 815-379-2155

President, Tony Zueger.

Visiting: Chalet Cheese and Gourmet Shop hours: 8:00 a.m.-5:00 p.m. all year, Monday-Saturday. Cheesemaking process can be seen from viewing area in the Swiss Chalet between 8:00 a.m. and 2:00 p.m. Monday through Friday.

Tours scheduled for large or small groups. Mail order cheese.

Directions: Walnut is in north-central Illinois, 40 miles east of Moline, 100 miles west of Chicago, on Rt. 92.

A handsome Swiss-style chalet is the home of Walnut Cheese Division of Avanti Foods. Avanti was founded, in 1964, to make and market Gino's Pizzas. Walnut Cheese was founded in 1932 and became a division of Avanti in 1972. The Swiss Chalet showcase was built in 1977. Six thousand pounds of cheese are made daily from local milk, and the varieties that need aging are kept here. Many different varieties of cheese are made, examples to be found in the gourmet shop, which sells cheese balls and cheese trays. Visitors are welcomed all year, any day except Sunday, when Avanti-Walnut is closed.

Kolb-Lena Cheese Company

301 West Railroad St., Lena, IL 60148

Phone: 815-369-4577

Owner, Frieda Renter; office manager, Dorothy Demeter.

Retail Shop Hours: Daily 8:30 a.m.-noon and 1:00 p.m.-5:00 p.m.; Saturday closed at 4:00 p.m. Mail orders.

Cheeses include brie, camembert, brick, Swiss, aged cheddar, Colby, blue, feta, and several others under Delico label.

Tours: Tuesday-Friday 9:00 a.m. for 8 people or more. Call in advance.

Directions: From north, Rt. 20, cross railroad tracks and turn right, 3 blocks. From south, Rt. 73, turn left before railroad tracks, 3 blocks.

When a Midwestern version of a celebrated French cheese is served regularly in fine, expensive restaurants in New York, Chicago, and other cities, there has to be a reason. There is. Excellent and dependable quality. Kolb-Lena's camembert and brie are well-known and often praised. Other fine cheeses are made by this firm as well.

Frederick Kolb, a German immigrant, founded the Kolb-Lena Cheese Company in 1925, choosing the location because of the high quality of milk produced there. Lena is more or less an extension of the cheese center of southwestern Wisconsin. It is only twenty miles from Monroe, Wisconsin's cheese capital.

Frieda Renter is the daughter of Frederick Kolb, and her daughter, Dorothy Demeter, is the third generation to be involved in the production of these fine cheeses.

Nauvoo Cheese Company

Nauvoo, IL 62354

Phone: 217-453-2213

Cheesemaker, Jim McCartey.

Blue cheese.

Retail cheese shop at the plant. Cheese also available by mail order.

Directions: Go east through Nauvoo; at St. Mary's Friary turn right, watch for signs.

Old breweries are favorite buildings for converting into wineries, but, because of the limestone caves, Oscar Rohde found the old Schenk Brewery (abandoned from Prohibition to 1937) an ideal place for making his blue cheese. Limestone caves are perfect for curing blue cheese. Rohde died in 1965, but his family continues to operate the cheese plant, and Nauvoo's blue cheese is one of the great ones of the world. It goes to many markets, but Los Angeles has a special yen for this flavorsome cheese, demanding a truckload every third week. The factory makes about three million pounds a year.

Old Man Mississippi is pretty impressive at Nauvoo; the river is very wide here.

The Cheeses
of Iowa

Iowa once was a cheesier state than it is now. The rich farm land is too valuable for corn and soybeans to permit much grazing of cattle. There *is* Iowa cheese, but you sometimes have to look for it. And it's strange how often "Iowa" cheese turns out to be Wisconsin cheese!

For example, Robert Lawlor, proprietor of Iowa's only conventional winery, Christina Wine Cellars, says that a number of excellent cheeses are made near Mc Gregor, "but they are on the Wisconsin side of the Mississippi." He mentions the Johnson family's fine cheddar made at Mt. Sterling and sold in their store, and the Lawlors' favorite Muenster cheese, made by the Schurman Brothers Cheese Factory at Lancaster, and sold there.

Few of the cheese factories in Iowa are equipped to greet visitors. The Ridgeway Dairy at Ridgeway, for example, produces 40,000 pounds of cheddar cheese daily except Sunday, and ships it as barrels of curd to the Borden Company, for further processing. And Schley Cheese Company at Cresco, in business for forty-seven years, makes 6,800 pounds of longhorn and curds every day, which they sell to Borden and John Morrell Company and to local groceries.

You can visit Maytag Dairy Farms at Newton, however, or order this excellent Iowa blue cheese.

The Goldfield Cheese Mart does a brisk retail and mail order business in Midwestern cheese, so we checked out their Iowa suppliers.

Goldfield Cheese Mart

Box 188, Goldfield, IA 50542

Phone: 515-825-3450

Visiting: 7:00 a.m.-5:00 p.m., 6 days a week.

Retail shop. Cheese also available by mail order.

Natural cheddar, swiss, Colby; cheese with salami, hot pepper, etc.

Directions: Highways 3 and 17.

This neat shop in northwestern Iowa sells Iowa, Minnesota, and Wisconsin cheese.

Some of the Iowa cheddar comes from Associated Milk Producers Inc. of Whittemore, owned by S.F. Howe of San Antonio, Texas. The factory at Whittemore makes 27,000 pounds of cheddar daily.

The other nearby Iowa cheese supplier to Goldfield is the Renwick Cheese Company.

Maytag Dairy Farms

Box 806, Newton, IA 50208

Phone: 515-792-1133

President, Donn M. Campbell.

Visiting: Monday-Friday 8:00 a.m.-5:00 p.m.; Saturday 9:00-1:00 p.m.

Retail shop, mail order.

Blue cheese, also Brick in the Round, cheddar, edam, Swiss.

Directions: North from I-80 on Rt. 14 just west of Newton, about 3 miles.

Maytag's famous blue cheese is made by a process developed at Iowa

State University. The Holstein-Friesian herd responsible for its quality grazes on 1,600 acres of land. The cheeses are aged in caves a minimum of six months before they're shipped to customers all over the United States and to foreign countries, with safe delivery guaranteed. Send for catalog to learn of prices, other products.

Renwick Cheese Company

(Renwick Creamery)
Renwick, IA 50577

Phone: 515-824-3631

Owner, Tom Gimer; head cheesemaker, Earl Nelson.

Retail Shop: 8:00 a.m.-5:00 p.m., 6 days a week.

Mail order sales.

Tours: Phone for information.

Longhorn, Monterey jack, edam, caraway, cheddar, Colby.

Directions: North and a little east of Fort Dodge. On Main Street. Signs point the way.

Tom Gimer's father was a buttermaker, and his wife's grandfather and great-grandfather were buttermakers. Butter and cheese production has decreased over the years because the flat land is better for raising grain crops than for grazing cows. But the Gimers, in the cheese business for twenty-five years, still make about 900,000 pounds annually and deliver it to stores themselves.

The Cheeses
of Michigan

Michigan is not famous for cheese; nevertheless, there are important cheese plants in the state. One of them is located at Michigan State University, East Lansing. Its importance is rather out of proportion to its size; a teaching and research cheesery, it produces 600 pounds of cheese a day, which scarcely bears comparison to the output of a commercial factory such as the Kraft plant at Pinconning where thousands of pounds of Colby, brick, Muenster, and Monterey jack are turned out. Pinconning has been famous for its Colby cheese since the early 1900's when Michigan cheese fanciers started calling it Pinconning cheese. You can still buy it at McCort's Cheese Store in Pinconning as earlier generations did.

Michigan did "invent" one cheese, farmer's cheese, a high protein, pressed cottage cheese originated in the town of Scottville. Scottville and Pinconning are across-state from one another, Scottville near the border of Lake Michigan, Pinconning in Saginaw Bay in Lake Huron.

At MSU's Dairy Plant, groups may see cheese being made by students of dairy science, and may purchase some of it. Dr. Ramesha Chandan, associate professor of Health Science and Nutrition, explains that as a teaching and research facility, the university cheesemaking plant is exempt from some of the restrictions on commercial plants which prevent opening them to tours. However, the tours must be strictly supervised for health and sanitation reasons.

Cheeses made at this "practice" plant include *degano*,* a very mild, nutty cheese with a texture similar to that of Swiss, which may be smoked or seasoned with caraway, and *rozano*, which is made with corn oil instead of milk for use in cholesterol-restricted diets. A super-nutritious, low-calorie chocolate cheese confection which tastes much like fudge is also made there, and is popular with students as a snack.

Other cheeses made and studied at MSU include cheddar, brick, and European types such as Holland's edam and gouda, Germany's tilsiter and Denmark's samsoe. Dr. Chandan told us of the importance of whey research at the university. Whey, while ninety-four percent water, is a serious water pollutant when poured down the drain or discharged into a lake. Cheese factories must dispose of millions of gallons of whey, and it is necessary to find uses for it, or to put it back into the food chain, Dr. Chandan said.

Whey cheese is made by the MSU plant, as well as ice cream and yogurt using whey solids. Research is being done on a sweetener which will be a lower-calorie sugar substitute.

Cheese may be purchased in the small salesroom at the model cheese plant. The best time for tours is in the morning at nine o'clock. Cheesemaking begins at seven and is finished by noon each day.

Call 517-355-8466 about a tour of the cheese plant.

Directions: The Dairy Plant is in Anthony Hall on Farm Lane and Wilson, next to the Food Science Building at MSU, East Lansing.

Copper Country Dairy, Inc.

Dollar Bay (Upper Peninsula), MI 49922

Phone: 906-482-3440

Manager, Surjit Kamra; cheesemaker, Wayne Kangas.

Cheeses: Cheddar, Colby, and Frankenmuth, a variety originated by and named for a Bavarian settlement in Michigan, once very popular.

Mail order cheese including Christmas box, but no retail sales.

Tours not on a regular basis. Phone for information.

* Developed by the Arthur Cheese Co. of Arthur, IL.

Copper Country Dairy is a cooperative of 120 farmers. Much of its product is sold to Kraft. The remainder is handled through a group of distributors and sold by mail order. Production is one million pounds per year.

Directions: Four miles from Michigan Technical University at Houghton. Immediately off Highway M-26, northeast of Houghton. There are signs.

Herbruck's Cheese Counter

2343 North U.S. 27, St. John's, MI 48879

Phone: 517-224-7396

Owners, Esther and Maynard Bailey.

200 varieties of cheese, gourmet foods, gift shop, lunch counter.

Michigan cheeses: Colby (Pinconning), specialties made by Bailey, degano from MSU.

Retail, wholesale, mail order, gift boxes.

Tours available on request. Open seven days a week: 7:00 a.m.-9:00 p.m. summer; 8:00 a.m.-8:00 p.m. winter.

Directions: 1¼ miles north of St. John's on U.S. 27.

Although Herbruck's modestly calls itself a cheese counter, it is really a full-fledged cheese store with rounds and blocks of cheddar and Colby aging in its cellar. Cheeses come from all over the world as well as Wisconsin, New York, and Michigan. Customers come for miles to this farming community to buy cheeses, fancy groceries, and to chat with the proprietors.

In addition to cheesemaking, the Baileys daily bake and sell doughnuts and homemade pies.

They sell up to 2,000 pounds of cheese a week to other markets across the country, as well as to local customers. The Baileys say they have over 2,000 gourmet items in their store including fish balls, sardines, mussels, smoked octopus, escargots, and fancy breads. Cheeses include salt-free, low cholesterol, corn oil, and goat cheeses for special diets.

Maynard Bailey studied cheesemaking at Michigan State in order to make his specialties, such as a really delicious chocolate cheese, fudgy but not too sweet, that put him on "What's My Line?" He makes strawberry and blueberry cheese, too, as well as spreads and nut-coated cheese balls.

Herbruck's was founded in 1922 by Mrs. Bailey's parents who sold dairy products from house to house.

Win Schuler's Bar-Scheeze

P.O. Box 104, Marshall, MI 49068.
Mail orders.

Win Schuler's Bar-Scheeze is now so well distributed that you may find it at your supermarket. United Airlines stewardesses have been bringing little containers of Bar-Scheeze with bread sticks to precede lunches or dinners in the "friendly skies." Of course you can eat this delectable, piquantly-seasoned cheese spread when you dine at any of the seven Win Schuler restaurants, or buy a crock of it to take home.

By Schuler's own account, the Bar-Scheeze was invented soon after he opened his first restaurant in Marshall, Michigan, in 1946. It was developed one evening at a small party when Schuler was experimenting with ingredients for a spread which would "soften" the pre-dinner drinks of old friend Duffy Daugherty, former Michigan State University football coach. After persistent "diddling," Win hit on a blend "so delicious that Duffy took to carting it home in ice cream containers."

The label indicates that the spread is made with cheddar cheese and salad dressing. There's horseradish in it along with other seasoners, but of course the formula is a family secret. We do know that it begins with forty-pound blocks of well-aged cheddar.

There's a Win Schuler Restaurant at Stevensville along I-94 close to Lakeside and Tabor Hill wineries. Chicagoans can stop there going to or coming from the wineries farther along, Bronte at Hartford, or the four at Paw Paw. The food and the comfortable, attractive setting are recommended as well as the famous Bar-Scheeze.

The Cheeses
of Missouri

Missouri is not thought of as a big cheese producer, but the state makes an important contribution to the nation's supply, specializing in cheddar and American longhorn. Many of the factories, such as the Greenfield Cheese Company at Greenfield, deliver what they make to Kraft Foods. The Mansfield Cheese Corporation doesn't even finish the cheese, delivering it as granular cheese to the big Kraft plant at Springfield for further processing.

The Springfield Kraft plant stores thirty million pounds of cheese in limestone caves, which keep the delicious stuff at proper room temperature for maturing. Some cheeses—limburger and Swiss, for example—require more chill than the natural cave temperature affords, so refrigeration is added to those tunnels where the limburger and Swiss are stored. Distribution is from the caves also.

We found two special cheesemaking plants to visit, both recommended by wineries that serve their cheese.

Mid-America Dairymen, Inc.

Emma, MO 65327

Phone: 816-463-2237

Manager, Homer Dierking; cheesemaker, Larry Haesemeier.

Hours: Daily 8:00 a.m.-5:00 p.m.; closed Sunday.

Retail sales.

Tours given for large groups. A week's notice required.

Directions: On I-70 about 60 miles east of Kansas City. In the middle of town on a crossroads.

When two wineries bragged about the cheese they serve with their wine-tastings and told us it came from the town of Emma, we put our sleuth to work. Sure enough, there was a cheddar cheese factory, right on the road to Kansas City, one which can be visited when you're on a winery tour. If you've purchased wines, here's where to find cheeses for enjoyable accompaniment.

Cheesemaker Haesemeier turns out 12-13,000 pounds a day.

The home office of Mid-America is at Springfield.

Stockton Cheese Company

Stockton, MO 65785

Phone: 417-276-3210

Owner, Calvin Johnson; Rudi Basecke, cheesemaker.

Hours: Daily 8:00 a.m.-5:00 p.m., Sunday 9:00 a.m.-5:00 p.m.

No tours.

Mail order sales; retail sales.

Directions: 1 mile east on 32 out of Stockton. Stockton is northwest of Springfield Lake.

In addition to American longhorn and cheddar cheese, you can buy honey, sorghum, sausage, and bric-a-brac at this cheese company's retail store. Rudi Basecke makes 5,300 to 6,000 pounds of cheese every day. A lot of it, when aged just right, goes UPS to cheese fanciers who order it.

The Cheeses
of Ohio

A Swiss colony that settled near Alliance, Ohio made the first Swiss cheese in America, and the state is still famous for its Swiss. There's an annual Swiss cheese festival in the Apple Creek area. The Brewster Dairy at Brewster makes excellent Swiss and has a reputation for it that reaches far beyond the boundaries of the state.

Colby and cheddar are favorite Ohio cheeses, too, and at Van Wert two special cheeses are made, camembert and Liederkranz, both by the Borden Company.

Liederkranz was developed by Emil Frey in Monroe, New York around 1892, and was named for a singing group, the Liederkranz Society. The name is now a registered trademark of the Borden Company, and the cheese, delicate when young, strong-flavored and strong-smelling when it has ripened fully, is made in Van Wert, along with camembert and limburger. Camembert is the wine cheese, while the stronger-flavored cheeses are more suitable for beer than wine.

Camembert originated in France, of course, and is associated with Marie Harel. Marie served it to Napoleon, who named the cheese for the commune of Camembert where he was stopping. If Marie Harel did not actually invent camembert, she at least made a particularly fine cheese of the kind. The farmers of the little Normandy town of Vimoutiers erected a statue to Marie Harel, but in June, 1944, a misdirected bomb dropped by the American Air Force destroyed the statue, symbol of one of the loved legends of France. Word got back to Ohio at the end of the war, and the employees of the camembert plant at Van Wert felt so bad about the bombing that they raised $2,000 for a new statue. A competition was conducted in France to choose the sculptor, and the new statue of Marie Harel was erected in 1956, as a gesture of good will.

Camembert is delicious with fruity red wines, and Ohio is a state that makes some good ones: baco noir, de Chaunac, chelois, and others.

Brewster Dairy, Inc.

Brewster, OH 54954

Phone: 216-767-3492

President, Fritz Leaman.

Restaurant; retail store; mail order cheese.

Directions: St. Rt. 39, in town.

You can buy a sandwich and a cup of coffee as well as cheese in this factory, which keeps three or four cheesemakers busy the year round. Produced are Swiss, Colby and processed cheese in 500-pound barrels.

Holmes Cheese Co.

Millersburg, OH 44654

Phone: 216-674-6451

Manager-President, R.J. Ramseyer; cheesemaker, Walter Ramseyer.

Retail salesroom at factory.

Directions: St. Rt. 39, one mile west of town.

This is a very up-to-date Swiss cheese factory with modern equipment. The cheese is made in closed kettles rather than the open kettles of former times. Cheese is made in 200-pound blocks at a rate of 16,000 pounds per day.

The Cheeses of Wisconsin

Wisconsin may not be very big on wineries, but cheese is another matter. The dairy state is one big cheesery, producing over a billion pounds of cheese a year, in 200 varieties! Think of all those cows!

Falls Dairy Company at tiny Jim Falls makes fifty-eight million pounds of cheddar a year, all for Kraft Foods, except for some the company buys back from Kraft to sell at the factory.

And talk about BIG! Some readers may remember the seventeen-and-a-quarter-ton cheese the state of Wisconsin exhibited at the New York World's Fair of 1964-65. After its two-year aging at the fair, the Big Cheese went on tour across the country, in its own cheesemobile, showing itself off at fairs, expositions, and shopping centers. And then the mammoth cheddar, ripe and tangy, was cut up and sold.

The super cheese, biggest ever made anywhere, was produced at the factory of Steve's Cheese Company, near Denmark, Wisconsin, by Steve Siudzinski, with the help of four other champion cheddar cheesemakers and the supplemental production of many other dairies and cheese factories.

After fifty-six years of making cheddar cheese in big sizes (no other size approaching seventeen tons!), Steve Siudzinski sold Steve's

Cheese to Lorance Raeder in 1976. It is now a division of Raeder's Branch Cheese Company of Branch, Wisconsin.

Monroe is the Swiss cheese center of Wisconsin. Green County, including the area around Monroe and New Glarus, was settled by Swiss immigrants in the middle of the nineteenth century. They brought their cheesemaking skills with them. The Swiss cheese made in that area is sweet and its eyes are the size of a cherry, as they should be; it is given a cure of at least six months, so that the characteristic flavor can develop. All cheese connoisseurs know that the best Swiss cheese is "grass" cheese, not winter cheese; it is made at the time of year when the cows are eating alfalfa. Yes, it's alfalfa, processed through the four stomachs of those brown and Holstein cows that makes the flavor difference!

You'll find other kinds of cheese in Green County, of course. It isn't all Swiss. But the ambience in the two towns certainly is. New Glarus is a typical Swiss village. Every year there's a Heidi festival and two William Tell performances on Labor Day weekend, one in German, one in English. There's good Swiss-German food in the restaurants, and shops sell marvelous sausages, pastries, antiques, and handmade articles.

Monroe calls itself the Swiss cheese capital of the United States. (So does a Swiss-influenced part of Ohio.) Thirty million pounds of Swiss are made annually in and around Monroe alone.

More Swiss cheese is made in the United States than in Switzerland!

One large cheese manufacturing company, Tolibia at Fond du Lac, which makes blue cheese, mozzarella, and provolone, apparently believed us to be spies out to discover their trade secrets, and we heard at least twenty times "I do not choose to divulge that information." Other plants will permit visitors to see their operations, which are usually behind glass in order to preserve the strict sanitary conditions under which cheese is made.

Along the well-traveled roads throughout the state, there are still small cheese factories that welcome visitors and may even offer samples. Almost always, they have not only their own cheese (cheddar or Colby or Swiss), but the cheeses of many other factories, too. Many do a good mail order business.

It would be impossible to list all of the cheese plants which have excellent products for sale, but here are some we can recommend. Prices are subject to variation (always upwards!), but a phone call or letter will give you current information, if you plan to order by mail.

Blaser's Alpine Cheese & Wine Haus, Inc.

Box 36, Comstock, WI 54826

Phone: 715-822-2437

Owner, Hermann Blaser.

Retail store; mail order sales.

Directions: Near Cumberland on Rt. 63, west and a little south of Rice Lake.

Hermann Blaser does a sizeable mail order and retail shop business with the cheese made in his Crystal Lake Cheese Factory. Bulk cheese is available in whatever size you want. Muenster, Wisconsin brick, Swiss, and medium or sharp cheddar can be purchased in bulk. Sharp cheddar is aged for two years, and has just the right crumbly snappishness.

Many other cheeses are available in smaller size packages—Colby, gouda, Swedish brick, Swedish brick caraway, salami cheese, and others. Beef summer sausage "from a little Swiss village in Wisconsin" and Wisconsin Maple Syrup are other goodies sold in and from Blaser's Alpine Cheese and Wine Haus. Just write and ask for details, or stop in when you're in northwest Wisconsin's lake-dotted resort country.

Chalet Cheese Cooperative

County Trunk N, Monroe, WI 53566

Phone: 608-325-4343

Manager, Albert Deppeler.

Factory store hours: Monday-Friday, 8:00 a.m.-3:30 p.m.

Tours by appointment.

Directions: From Monticello, west on C 4 miles to N, south 5 miles on N.

Chalet's setting is picturesque and reminds you of Switzerland. In 1887, there were five farmer members of this cooperative; today there are fifty-two. Swiss cheese was made until the thirties, then a switch was made to limburger. The present building was constructed in 1947, with limburger in mind.

Chalet makes one-and-one-half-million pounds of limburger a year, to sell under several labels, plus 700,000 pounds each of brick and cheddar. There are more than 100 distributors of Chalet Cheese.

Elm Dairy Cooperative Assn.

Coleman, WI 54112

Phone: 414-897-3352

Manager-cheesemaker, Alvin Zahn; cheesemaker, Craig Goldsmith.

Retail store in factory.

Tours by appointment. New facilities.

Directions: Coleman is directly north of Green Bay on US 141, beyond Lena, another cheese town. Approaching from the south, turn right (east) on M (look for Old Schoolhouse Antique shop), 5 miles east on M. On left.

Alvin Zahn is a friendly, welcoming man, full of stories about cheese. He has been with the Co-op forty years. Organized in 1916, the Elm Dairy Cooperative consists of forty-four farmer members. Distributors are Frigo Cheese Corporation and County Line Cheese. Daily production: 2,500 pounds of cheddar cheese.

Falls Dairy Company

Jim Falls, WI 54748

Phone: 715-382-4113

Owners, DEC International; president and chief executive officer, Ray Rogers; president of Falls Dairy, Ervin Purdeu. Five cheesemakers.

Retail cheese sales from 8:00 a.m.-4:30 p.m. No mail orders.

Tours by appointment (for people not in the cheese business).

Directions: 12 miles north of Chippewa Falls on 178. Watch for signs.

Wouldn't it be worth the trip just to have a look at a cheese factory running non-stop day and night that turns out *fifty-eight million pounds* of cheddar a year? It's the biggest cheese factory in the United States and possibly the world.

Klondike Cheese Cooperative

Monroe, WI 53566

Phone: 608-325-3021

Managers, A.S. Buholzer and Sons, Inc.; cheesemakers, Ronald and Steven Buholzer; bookkeeper, Rosa Buholzer.

Retail sales at the Junction House, a neighborhood, family-owned tavern.

No tours.

Cheeses: Monterey jack, Colby, Muenster, cheddar, and curds. Wholesale only at factory.

Directions to the Junction House: On Highway 81 west of Monroe toward Argyle.

Klondike Cheese Cooperative has been run by the Buholzer family for three generations. Rosa Buholzer's father, Albert Vogel, was a cheesemaker in Switzerland before he came to Wisconsin. The Buholzer sons start the cheesemaking at 1:30 a.m. and finish by eight o'clock. The Junction House, where Klondike cheese is available, is one of the oldest buildings in the area. In the 1860's, it was a farmer's market, stable, and tavern. During Prohibition, it became a dance hall with a trap door to conceal the goings-on below, where applejack, wine, and other illegal "booze" was available.

Nowadays you can play pool, have a hamburger, buy Klondike Cheese, or have a legal drink at the Junction House.

How Klondike got its name: The plant was once the Stauffacher Factory which burned to the ground during the time of the Klondike Gold rush. The farmers who rebuilt it decided to call it Klondike.

Kugel's Cheese Mart

Lena, WI 54139

Phone: 414-829-5537

Owners: Jim and Karen Kugel.

Retail store for Frigo Cheese Corporation.

Cheese: Over 60 varieties including blue, fontina, fontinella, provolone, romano, parmesan, asiago, ricotta and others. Wines also for sale.

Mail orders.

Directions: On Highway 141; Lena is north of Green Bay.

Frigo Cheese Corporation, which has several subsidiaries in Wisconsin and Michigan, doesn't receive visitors or offer tours, but this retail shop carries all the cheeses, many of them Italian types. Kugel's also sells cheeses from other Wisconsin producers, and several imported cheeses as well. Sausages, maple syrup, and a few other food items are available here, too—enough to make a good picnic. The shop is right next door to Frigo.

Merkt's Cheese Store

(Retail outlet and mail order store for Merkt Cheese Company, Inc.)

P.O. Box 337, Salem, WI 53168

Phone: 414-843-2424

Owner, Tom Merkt.

Hours: 9:00 a.m.-6:00 p.m. seven days a week.

Kinds of cheese: cheddar spread and 8 different variations: bacon, brandy, garlic, horseradish, toasted onions, pepper, smoked, wine. Swiss spread, 3 variations: almond, blue cheese, cherry. Also for sale, Merkt's pork-liver sausage.

Directions: From Chicago I-94 to 50, left at Hwy. 83, ½ mi. to Salem, 5 mi. north of Antioch.

Merkt Cheese Company, Inc.

(Manufacturers of Bristol Club Cold Pack Cheese Food)

P.O. Box 22, 19241-83rd St., Bristol, WI 53104

Phone: 414-857-7011

Co-owners, Carol M. Merkt-Wilks, Tom Merkt.

Hours: 8:00 a.m.-4:30 p.m. five days a week.

Directions: From Chicago I-94 to 50, left at Hwy. 45, ½ mi. to Bristol.

Merkt's Cheese Store, where you can send for the cheese if your cheese market doesn't have it, is at Salem, which is close to Bristol but may not be on your map, for it's even smaller than Bristol. Merkt's Bristol Club cheese comes in many combinations: with wine, with brandy, with bacon or almonds or garlic. There's also a cheddar with pepper, and a Swiss with chives.

When you make a better cheese to bait a better mousetrap, lots of people will beat a path to your door. Actually, Carol Merkt's Bristol Club Cheese is too good for mice! The Merkt spreads are made with top quality cheddar or Swiss cheese as a base. Mrs. Merkt buys her cheddar from Outagamie Cheese Cooperative, at Black Creek, and the Swiss from Green County Cheese of Monroe, otherwise known as Swiss Colony.

Mrs. Merkt makes her delicious cheese mixtures without preservatives, but they keep well because you can freeze and refreeze them in their plastic containers.

Carol Merkt's late husband, George, thought up the idea of Bristol Club Cold Pack Cheese Food. The business has grown by word of mouth, and Mrs. Merkt sold the retail and mail order business to her nephew Tom Merkt, to be able to concentrate on the manufacturing process. Mrs. Merkt says she wants to stay a small company, so as not to be gobbled by a conglomerate. However, the business keeps growing—in 1978 she made well over two million pounds of Merkt's Bristol Club Cold Pack Cheese. That says something for Carol Merkt's cheese specialty!

Outagamie Cheese Cooperative

Black Creek, WI 54106

Phone: 414-984-3331

Manager, Laverne Swensen; assistant manager, Thomas Ebert; foreman, Ray Palubicki.

Cheddar, Colby, brick, edam, low-sodium cheddar and Colby, caraway, garlic cheese.

Retail sales at factory; mail orders.

Tours no longer available.

Directions: In town, on Highway 54.

Outagamie Cheese Cooperative consists of 340 farmers. Nine cheese-makers turn out 60,000 to 65,000 pounds daily, most of which goes to Safeway Stores, Inc.

About twenty-five per cent of the milk brought to the co-op is sent to Chicago as Grade A quality milk. Outagamie employs sixty-five full-time workers and ten part-time, quite a change since six farmers bought a bankrupt creamery, in 1932, and turned it into Outagamie Cheese Cooperative!

Renard's Rosewood Dairy

Algoma, WI 54201

RENARD'S Cloverleaf Dairy

Nasewaupee, WI 54235

Phone: Rosewood, 414-743-6626; Cloverleaf, 414-825-7272

Owners, Howard and Gary Renard.

Retail sales at both locations, Monday-Friday, 8:00 a.m.-5:00 p.m.; Saturday, 8:00 a.m.-3:00 p.m. Closed Sunday.

Cheddar, Colby, Muenster, Swiss, caraway, mozzarella, farmer's cheese, limburger, many others. Fresh curds daily. Wine.

Tours: (Rosewood) 9:00 a.m.-noon. Large tours by arrangement.

Directions to Rosewood: 5½ miles north of Algoma on Highway S.

Directions to Cloverleaf: 7 miles south of Sturgeon Bay on Highway 57.

Door County attracts thousands of tourists, which is why Howard and Angela Renard and son Gary and his wife Bonnie opened a second

Cloverleaf "dairy." It is really an extension of Rosewood, where the men make their cheese. The Cloverleaf, and "the Cheddar Box," adjacent to the Rosewood factory, now sell wines as well as cheese. The cheeses made here are cheddar, Colby, brick, and Muenster, but many others are available in the two shops. Sausage also is available.

The factory has been producing cheese since 1915 (it burned down and was rebuilt). The Renards have owned it since 1961; 10,000 pounds are produced daily.

Ryser's Cheese and Gift Chalet

209 E. Main St., Mt. Horeb, WI 53572

Phone: 608-437-3051

Owner, Ryser Bros. of Wisconsin (factory); cheesemaker, Luther Severson.

Cheddar, brick, caraway brick, beer cheese, Colby, Muenster, Monterey jack, Swiss, pallatelle, farmer's cheese.

Mail order.

No tours, but you can watch champion cheesemakers at work through a large window.

Directions: Mt. Horeb is 15 miles west of Madison on Highway 18. Ryser's is in the middle of town.

Cheese is not the only business of Ryser Brothers, wholesale food provisioners based in Chicago. Their Cheese and Gift Chalet is cannily planted on Main Street, in a small town well oriented to tourist interests. There are antique shops and good places to eat in Mt. Horeb. Cave of the Mounds, well worth seeing, is only five miles away, and the Tyrol Basin Ski Area is near. Best of all, perhaps, Mt. Horeb and Prairie du Sac are not far apart, and at Prairie du Sac, or rather near it, we find the Wollersheim Winery.

The Chalet sells Ryser's and other cheeses, plus crackers to go with cheese, and sausage, candy, jellies and jams, maple syrup, coffee beans to grind yourself, beer steins, clocks, and bric-a-brac. Lots of good touristy stuff.

There are ten choices in gift packages at a wide range of prices.

Springside Cheese Factory, Inc.

Rt. 1, Coleman, WI 54112

Phone: 414-897-3075

Owner-Cheesemaker, Wayne Hintz.

Cheddar, Colby.

Retail cheese sold at the factory. Open "early" 7 days a week in summer; closed Sundays in winter. No mail order sales.

Tours: Call to make arrangements.

Directions: From Coleman, take B west toward Klondike 6 miles. Turn left at sign "Kelly" (Kelly is a lake) 3½ miles, right side of road.

Wayne Hintz, a young cheesemaker, bought this factory several years ago, and with six employees produces 2,500 pounds of cheese a day, ninety percent of which goes to Wisconsin Northern Produce, Manitowoc. The rest is sold retail. Our scouts report that Springside is a very friendly place, and tell us the fresh cheese curds are particularly delicious. Where the curds are good the cheese is too!

Steve's Cheese Company

(Division Branch Cheese Co., Branch) Rt. 2, Denmark, WI 54208

Phone: 414-863-2397

Owner, Lorance Raeder; head cheesemaker, Darwin DeGrave.

Retail store next to factory sells cheddar, American, and Colby cheese. Mail order sales.

Tours in summer by arrangement, usually for bus loads of people.

Directions: Three miles north of Denmark on 141. Follow signs. On the way to Green Bay.

Don't miss having a look at the factory that made the world's biggest cheddar, when you're in the Green Bay area, or on your way to the famous Door County Peninsula, Wisconsin's favorite summer resort where fishing, sailing, antiquing, and cherry-picking are some of the recreations.

Steve's turns out 12,000 pounds of cheese a day for Borden's, Wilson, Topko, and Wisconsin Produce, keeping out enough to stock the retail store and take care of the mail order business. The sharp cheddar (two years old) is excellent. Of course the other cheeses such as caraway, blue, edam, and Steve's aged cheese spread are sold as well. Local sausages, Wisconsin honey, and maple syrup are also available. Gift boxes are available mail order at a wide price range. Write for a brochure.

Swiss Cheese Shop and Demonstration Factory

Box 4292, Monroe, WI 53566

Phone: 608-325-3493

Manager, Archie Meyers.

Other premises at Janesville and Beloit.

Lecture and movie on cheesemaking followed by tasting. Programs (50 minutes) start 10 minutes after the hour, every hour between 9:00 a.m. and 5:00 p.m. There is a small charge.

Retail cheese. Gift shop (lederhosen and Tyrolean hats!). Open 8:00 a.m.-6:00 p.m.

Directions: One and a quarter miles north of Monroe on Highway 69.

Here's where to go if you want to see the cheese process from start to finish, and then taste some cheeses. The factory is simulated. All processes are shown, but the cheese is fake. The samples are real though. You can buy real cheese, too: Swiss, cheddar, Colby, Muenster, Monterey jack, brick, limburger, spreads, and other kinds of cheese.

Sausage, candy, knick-knacks, and gifts are sold here. As many as 150 people can see the "cheesemaking" at one time.

Cheese gift packs available.

Thiel's Wisconsin Cheese House

(Thiel's Milk Products, Inc.)

(St. John) Rt. 2, Hilbert, WI 54129

Phone: 414-989-1440

Owner, Kenneth Thiel.

Bulk cheddar, cheddar, spreads, Colby, brick.

Retail sales; mail order sales.

Directions: Center of four highways, 10, 114, 57 and 55.

Thiel's specializes in cold pack crock cheese in "junior" (20 ounces) or "giant" (40 ounces) sizes. They also sell a variety of cheddar spreads, including smoked, and flavored with port wine. Natural cheese may be purchased mild, medium, or sharp.

The store also offers a selection of cheeses from other plants and sells jellies, crackers, sausage, and gifts.

Wheel of Swiss Chateau

657 2nd St., Monroe, WI 53566

Phone: 608-328-4151

Owners, Mr. and Mrs. John Marty; cheesemaker, Duane Torkelson.

Hours: Weekdays, 9:00 a.m.-5:00 p.m.; Sunday, 11:00 a.m.-5:00 p.m. Tours by arrangement, no Sunday tours.

Retail shop; mail order cheese.

Directions: Junction of Highway 69 bypass and Highway 81. Other premises at Browntown, several miles west on State Highway 11.

Here's the place to get a good look at cheesemaking! The handsome Wheel of Swiss Chateau which turns out six wheels or blocks of Swiss cheese daily, each weighing 160 to 180 pounds, has provided glassed-in walkways from which visitors can see cheese being made.

The retail store sells not only the Marty Swiss, mild, medium, or aged, but many other cheeses, including caraway brick, lager brick (beer cheese), camembert, brie, Muenster, garlic cheddar, smoked Swiss or cheddar, hot pepper cheese, and others. Also local sausages and Carol Merkt's delicious cold pack cheese spread.

Local residents sell their handicraft here, too.

White Clover Dairy, Inc.

Kaukauna, WI 54130

Phone: 414-766-3517

Vice-president of production, Bernard ("Butch") Fasbender.

Cheese sold retail, no mail order.

No tours.

Edam, gouda, Muenster, farmer's cheese.

Directions: I-94 to 141, to 57, north off 57 on Highway D 3 miles.

This factory is one of the major producers of Holland type cheeses, and with its associated plant, the Pussini Cheese Factory at Cascade, which makes Italian-type provolone, mozzarella, and parmesan, is major supplier to the cheese counters of Wisconsin, in the private label cheese business.

The factory was privately owned from 1920 to 1947, when it was incorporated. The Nestlé Company has recently purchased both plants, whose combined output is twelve million pounds of cheese annually.

About the Author

RUTH ELLEN CHURCH is one of the country's most widely known and highly respected wine writers. For many years she was wine columnist as well as food editor of the *Chicago Tribune*. She is author of a baker's dozen books on food and wine. Most wine buffs are familiar with her pioneering wine book *The American Guide to Wines* and the more recent *Entertaining with Wine*. A slim, inexpensive volume which she wrote for *Better Homes and Gardens, Favorite American Wines and How to Enjoy Them*, won a "gold vine" award as best wine book of 1979.

In WINES OF THE MIDWEST, the author takes you on a tour of Midwestern wineries, most of them small farm wineries, revealing fascinating information about both wineries and winemakers. In this book she writes of the steadily improving wines of Illinois, Indiana, Iowa, Kentucky, Michigan, Minnesota, Missouri, Ohio and Wisconsin, with several peeks into adjacent areas—a dip into Arkansas, a continuing tour of Lake Erie wineries, four in North East Pennsylvania, and four more in New York.

Ruth Ellen Church knows that cheese is wine's best friend, so she invites the reader to step into some famous and little known Midwestern cheeseries, as well.

Publications of Interest

Journals and Magazines

American Wine Society Journal (a quarterly publication)

4218 Rosewold Ave.
Royal Oak, MI 48073

Subscription with membership in American Wine Society, $15.00.
The magazine carries notes from the various chapters of the Society, together with articles on various aspects of wine and wine-growing, frequently of a technical nature, and with particular emphasis on the eastern half of the United States.

The non-profit Society conducts an annual conference for amateur and professional winemakers, wine educators, and hobbyists, and publishes bulletins on such specialized subjects as grafting, pruning, malolactic fermentation, and wine-tastings. Audio-visual aids in teaching about wine are available through the Society. Margaret Jackisch is executive secretary.

American Wine Society Publications (order from above address)

"Still Wine from Grapes," Phillips, $2.00
"Making Wine at Home," Cornell, $2.00
"Sensory Identification of Wine Constituents," Jackisch, $2.00
"Guide to Winegrape Growing," McGrew, $2.50
Other titles available. Ask for list.

Eastern Grape Grower and Winery News

Box 329, Watkins Glen, N.Y. 14891
Subscription, 6 issues, $9.00

The publication reports news of wines and wineries, carries articles on grape-growing, grower problems such as vine diseases and air pollution, and sponsors an annual seminar and Eastern wine competition called Wineries Unlimited. Publisher, J. William Moffett.

Wine East

L and H Photojournalism, 620 N. Pine St., Lancaster, PA 17603
Bi-monthly magazine, $10.00

While the articles in this publication mainly concern eastern wineries and growers, much of the subject matter has broader appeal. Editors, Hudson Cattell and Lee Stauffer Miller.

L and H Photojournalism Publications (order from above address)
The Wines of the East

"The Hybrids," $2.75 plus 50 cents postage
"The Vinifera," $2.75 plus 50 cents postage
"Native American Grapes," $2.75 plus 50 cents postage
All three books, $7.50 plus $1.00 postage.

Wines and Vines

The Hiaring Company, 703 Market St., San Francisco, CA 94103
Subscription, 12 issues $18; with annual directory of wineries, $28.50.

This magazine carries dozens of news briefs about happenings in the industry, and both news and technical articles of interest to those in the wine business and associated enterprises. The directory lists all of the wineries in the country plus those of Canada and Mexico, naming their officers and wine brands and stating other pertinent information. *Wines and Vines* describes itself as "the authoritative voice of the grape and wine industry," which it most certainly is. Editor and publisher, Philip Hiaring.

Books

The Wines of America, by Leon Adams, McGraw-Hill Book Company, New York, $14.95.

Adams is the peripatetic traveler to the vineyards of this continent, well-known, much-admired, and respected. He has been a force in moving the American wine industry forward from the time he helped establish the California Wine Institute shortly after the end of Prohibition until today, when he is actively prodding to get antiquated, restrictive wine laws off the books of various states to permit the establishment of small wineries and freer marketing practices for wines. Adams's book, a thoroughly revised and expanded edition, is a basic resource for any wine buff. It covers the wineries of our country and those of our Canadian and Mexican neighbors in a most readable, lively fashion.

Grapes into Wine, by Philip M. Wagner, Alfred A. Knopf, New York, 1976, paperback, $6.95.

Subtitled "The Art of Winemaking in America," this book is a completely rewritten, up-to-date version of Wagner's well-known *American Wines and Winemaking*, the book that led so many of the winery owners represented in this volume into their careers. It is a valuable resource book and of much interest to the wine buff. Wagner and his wife Jocelyn are proprietors of Boordy Vineyard, Riderwood, Maryland. They have made wines and grown nursery stock for many years, and were the first to grow French-American hybrids commercially in the United States.

A Wine-Grower's Guide, revised edition, 1965, by Philip M. Wagner, Alfred A. Knopf, New York, $10.95.

This is the companion volume to *Grapes into Wine*, which guides the amateur into selecting and growing suitable grapes for his vineyard, training, pruning vines, contending with vineyard pests such as birds, animals, and insects, and propagation of vines.

Jefferson and Wine: *Thomas Jefferson: The Wine Connoisseur and Wine Grower,*   The Plains, Va. 22171. Edited by R. de Treville Lawrence, Sr. Paperback $4.50, hardcover $7.95.

The bicentennial book on Jefferson and his interest in wines is the work of the Vinifera Wine Growers Association. It is a collection of articles about Jefferson and wine and includes the Adlum correspondence regarding wines and vine cuttings supplied by Adlum to Thomas Jefferson.

The Vinifera Wine Growers Association publishes a journal, 3 issues a year, which comes with membership of $10.

Home Winemaker's Handbook, by Walter S. Taylor and Richard P. Vine, Harper and Row, New York.

You may have to search for this book, for it is out of print. But it is an excellent, practical guide to winemaking by the proprietor of Bully Hill Vineyards in Hammondsport, New York and the former winemaker-vice-president of Warner Vineyards in Paw Paw, Michigan.

The Ohio Winemakers, A History of the Early Days, A Tour Guide for Today, by Marshall C. Harrold. This 58-page booklet contains interesting historical material about Ohio wineries and takes the reader on a tour of some of Ohio's current wineries. Available from Marshall C. Harrold, 3031 Fairmont Ave., Dayton, OH, 45429. Price: $2. Add 50¢ mailing charge.

Specialists in Hard-to-Find Wine and Food Books

Eleanor Lowenstein*
Corner Book Shop
102 Fourth Ave.
New York, NY 10003

Elisabeth Woodburn
Booknoll Farm
Hopewell, NJ 08525

Jan Longone
The Wine and Food Library
1207 West Madison
Ann Arbor, MI 48103
(By mail or appointment; catalog $1)

* Since the death of the proprietor, this shop is open only from 1:00 p.m. to 3:00 p.m. daily. Inquire by mail or phone 212-254-7714 or 254-5998.

Index of Names

Index of Wineries

f = food such as cheese, sausage, pizza available
* = restaurant at the winery
p = picnic facilities available
w = winegarden or weinstube

Index of Cheeseries

Avanti Foods, Walnut Cheese Division, IL, 205

Blaser's Alpine Cheese and Wine Haus, Inc., WI, 229
Borden Company, The, IA, 209, 223
Brewster Dairy, Inc., OH, 224

Chalet Cheese Cooperative, WI, 229
Copper Country Dairy, Inc., WI, 214
County Line Cheese Company, WI, 230

Elm Dairy Cooperative Assn., WI, 230

Falls Dairy Company, WI, 231
Frigo Cheese Corporation, WI, 230

Goldfield Cheese Mart, IA, 209, 210
Greenfield Cheese Company, MO, 219

Herbruck's Cheese Counter, MI, 215
Holmes Cheese Company, OH, 224

Johnson Family, WI, 209

Klondike Cheese Cooperative, WI, 231
Kolb-Lena Cheese Company, IL, 206
Kraft Foods, 213, 215, 219, 227
Kugel's Cheese Mart, WI, 232

Mansfield Cheese Corporation, MO, 219
Maytag Dairy Farms, IA, 209, 210
McCort's Cheese Store, MI, 213
Merkt Cheese Company, WI, 233
Merkt's Cheese Store, WI, 233
Michigan State University, MI, 214
Mid-American Dairymen, Inc., MO, 220
Morrell Company, John, IA, 209

Nauvoo Cheese Company, IL, 207

Outagamie Cheese Cooperative, WI, 234

Raeder's Branch Cheese Company, WI, 228
Renard's Rosewood Dairy, WI, 235
Renwick Cheese Company, IN, 211
Ridgeway Dairy, IA, 209
Ryser's Cheese and Gift Chalet, WI, 236

Schurman Bros., WI, 209
Springside Cheese Factory, Inc., WI, 237
Steve's Cheese Company, WI, 237
Stockton Cheese Company, MO, 220
Swiss Cheese Shop and Demonstration Factory, WI, 238

Thiel's Wisconsin Cheese House, WI, 239

Wheel of Swiss Chateau, WI, 240
White Clover Dairy, Inc., WI, 240
Win Schuler's Bar-Scheeze, MI, 216